F. K. (Frank Key) Howard

Fourteen months in American bastiles

F. K. (Frank Key) Howard

Fourteen months in American bastiles

ISBN/EAN: 9783741182280

Manufactured in Europe, USA, Canada, Australia, Japa

Cover: Foto ©Andreas Hilbeck / pixelio.de

Manufactured and distributed by brebook publishing software
(www.brebook.com)

F. K. (Frank Key) Howard

Fourteen months in American bastiles

𝔉𝔬𝔲𝔯𝔱𝔢𝔢𝔫 𝔐𝔬𝔫𝔱𝔥𝔰

IN

AMERICAN BASTILES.

Frank A. Howard

"*It*" (*free speech*) "*is a homebred right—a fireside privilege. It has ever been enjoyed in every house, cottage and cabin in the nation. It is not to be drowned in controversy. It is as undoubted as the right of breathing the air and walking on the earth. It is a right to be maintained in peace and in war. It is a right which cannot be invaded without destroying constitutional liberty. Hence this right should be guarded and protected by the freemen of this Country with a jealous care, unless they are prepared for chains and anarchy.*"

[DANIEL WEBSTER.

"*Say at once that a free Constitution is no longer suitable to us ; say at once, in a manly manner, that, upon an ample review of the state of the world, a free Constitution is not fit for you ; conduct yourselves at once as the Senators of Denmark ; lay down your freedom, and acknowledge and accept of despotism. But do not mock the understandings and feelings of mankind by telling the world that you are free,—by telling me that if, for the purpose of expressing my sense of the public administration of this country, of the calamities which this war has occasioned, I state a grievance, or make any declaration of my sentiments in a manner that may be thought seditious, I am to be subjected to penalties hitherto unknown to the law.*"

[CHARLES JAMES FOX.

BALTIMORE:

PUBLISHED BY KELLY, HEDIAN & PIET,

No. 174 BALTIMORE STREET,

1863.

PREFACE.

THE unlawful and oppressive acts of Mr. LINCOLN, his advisers, and subordinates, during the war between this Government and that of the Confederate States, will hereafter constitute no insignificant portion of the history of these times. As one of the victims of the despotism, which he succeeded in maintaining, in the Northern and Border States, for so long a period, I desire to add my testimony to that which has been heretofore furnished, in relation to the outrages perpetrated under his Administration; and I give publicity to this statement now, while the facts are fresh in the recollection of the public, lest any one should at some remoter period venture to doubt its accuracy. I do not propose to discuss the absurdity of the theories on which Mr. LINCOLN claimed to exercise arbitrary power, nor the imbecility of his course. It is proper, however, in giving an account of the treatment to which, in common with hundreds of other men, I was subjected, to refer briefly to the position of affairs in Maryland, and the object of Mr. LINCOLN in inflicting on myself and my fellow sufferers the indignities and wrongs which we so long endured. Up to the time when the dissolution of the Union became, to most intelligent men, a patent fact, the people of Maryland had unanimously desired and striven for its perpetuation. Though they feared that the aggressive principles and growing power of the Republican party would, before many years, bring about a separation of the two sections of the country, and though they believed that the conduct of Mr. LINCOLN and his party justified the action of the South, they still hoped and labored for the maintenance of the Union. They earnestly desired that some compromise should be proposed by Congress, which would restore peace between the two sections, and they believed that such a settlement could readily be effected. When Congress refused to make any effort in that direction, they looked to what was called the "Peace Conference" to recommend some plan by which all dissensions might be healed. When all these hopes were disappointed by the action of Northern men, and especially when Mr. Lincoln, on his accession to office, appointed some of the most extreme partisans to high office at home, and selected others to represent the country abroad, and gave ample evidence of his incapacity to understand the questions at issue, and of his determination neither to conciliate the Southern people, nor to deal with what he called the "rebellion" according to the mode provided by the Constitution and laws, then a large proportion of the people of Maryland expressed their sympathy for the South, and their conviction of the justice of its cause. They then asserted that the conquest of the South was an impossibility, that the Union was in point of fact dissolved, and they insisted that in such case the people of the State had the right to decide their own destiny for themselves. These views I also entertained and expressed, as one of the editors of a Baltimore journal "The *Daily Exchange.*" But neither I, nor those who were afterwards my fellow prisoners, ever violated in any way, the Constitution or the laws. We defended the rights of our State, and criticized the policy of the Administration at Washington. We advanced our views with perfect freedom, as we had the right to do, and we did no more. But Mr. Lincoln had determined to suppress everything like free speech, not only in Maryland, but throughout the North. He had made up his mind that he would carry out his own projects irrespectively of the laws, or his constitutional obligations. Having therefore introduced Northern troops into the city of Baltimore and various parts of the State, and having fortified numerous points so far as to render resistance unavailing, he proceeded to execute his schemes. The Commissioners and Marshal of Police were arrested in Baltimore, and

5

the Police force was disbanded. Many of the most prominent members of the Legislature, on the eve of the meeting
of that body, the Mayor of Baltimore, and one the members
of Congress for that city, were arrested at midnight, and
dragged off to prison. Editors and other private citizens
were also among the proscribed. Newspapers were sup-
pressed, and the functions of the State and Municipal authorities usurped or suspended by agents of the Administration. Neither against me nor the vast majority of my
fellow prisoners did the officers of the Government ever
venture to prefer any specific charge. We were arrested
simply for daring to defend our unquestionable rights and
to exercise the liberty of free speech. Under these circumstances, it might have been supposed that we would be
treated with some regard to our health and comfort. As
we were detained, as was frequently admitted by Government officials, only as a precautionary measure, it might
have been expected that those who chose to perpetrate so
gross a wrong, would at least recognize the right of inno-
cent and honorable men under such circumstances to be
considerately or decently dealt with. I do not propose, as I
have said, to discuss the enormity of the outrage inflicted
on us, or to measure the infamy which will attach to those
who were the authors or agents of that wrong. I only
wish to show now how men, who were guiltless of any
offence whatever, and who had been thrown into prison
because of their political opinions, were treated in this age,
and in this country. I submit the facts to the public, with
the assertion that the fairness and accuracy of my statement
cannot be successfully challenged. As I have not intended,
in the ensuing pages, to discuss the cases of "political
prisoners" generally, but merely to detail, in the form of
a personal narrative, my own experiences, I have been compelled to speak mainly of myself. Under these circumstances, this continual reference to my own views and situation has been unavoidable.

F. K. HOWARD.

BALTIMORE, *December*, 1862.

Fort McHenry.

On the morning of the 13th of September, 1861, at my residence in the city of Baltimore, I was awakened about 12½ or 1 o'clock, by the ringing of the bell. On going to the window, I saw a man standing on the steps below, who told me he had a message for me from Mr. S. T. WALLIS. I desired to know the purport of it, when he informed me that he could only deliver it to me privately. As it had been rumored that the Government intended to arrest the members of the Legislature, and as Mr. WALLIS was one of the most prominent of the Delegates from the City of Baltimore, I thought it probable that the threatened outrage had been consummated, and I hurried down to the door. When I opened it, two men entered, leaving the door ajar. One of them informed me that he had an order for my arrest. In answer to my demand that he should produce the warrant or order under which he was acting, he declined to do so, but said he had instructions from Mr. SEWARD, the Secretary of State.

I replied that I could recognize no such authority, when he stated that he intended to execute his orders, and that resistance would be idle, as he had a force with him sufficient to render it unavailing. As he spoke, several men entered the house, more than one of whom were armed with revolvers, which I saw in their belts. There was no one in the house when it was thus invaded, except my wife, children and servants, and under such circumstances, I of course, abandoned all idea of resistance. I went into my library and sent for my wife, who soon joined me there, when I was

2

8

informed that neither of us would be permitted to leave the room until the house had been searched. How many men were present, I am unable to say, but two or three were stationed in my library, and one at the front door, and I saw several others passing, from time to time, along the passage. The leader of the gang then began to search the apartment. Every drawer and box was thoroughly ransacked, as also were my portfolio and writing desk, and every other place that could possibly be supposed to hold any papers. All my private memoranda, bills, note-books, and letters were collected together to be carried off. Every room in the house subsequently underwent a similar search. After the first two rooms had been thus searched, I was told that I could not remain longer, but must prepare to go to Fort McHenry. I went up stairs to finish dressing, accompanied by the leader of the party, and I saw that men were stationed in all parts of the house, one even standing sentinel at the door of my children's nursery. Having dressed and packed up a change of clothes and a few other articles, I went down into the library, and was notified that I must at once depart. I demanded permission to send for my wife's brother or father, who were in the immediate neighborhood, but this was refused. My wife then desired to go to her children's room, and this request was also refused. I was forced to submit, and ordering my servants to remain in the room with my wife, and giving decided expression to my feelings concerning the outrage perpetrated upon me, and the miserable tyrants who had authorized it, I got into the carriage which was waiting to convey me to Fort McHenry. Two men, wearing the badges of the police force which the Government had organized, escorted me to the Fort. It was with a bitter pang that I left my house in possession of the miscreants who had invaded it. I afterwards learned that the search was continued for some time, and it was not until after 3 o'clock in the morning that they left the premises.

I reached Fort McHenry about 2 o'clock in the morning. There I found several of my friends, and others were brought in a few minutes afterwards. One or two were brought in later in the day, making fifteen in all. Among them were most of the Members of the Legislature from Baltimore, Mr. Brown, the Mayor of the City, and one of our Representatives in Congress, Mr. May. They were all gentlemen of high social position, and of unimpeachable character, and each of them had been arrested, as has been said, solely on account of his political opinions, no definite charge having been then, or afterwards, preferred against them. Two small rooms were assigned us during our stay. In the smaller one of these I was placed, with three companions. The furniture consisted of three or four chairs and an old ricketty bedstead, upon which was the filthiest apology for a bed I ever saw. There was also a tolerably clean looking mattress lying in one corner. Upon this mattress, and upon the chairs and bedstead, we vainly tried to get a few hours sleep. The rooms were in the second story of the building, and opened upon a narrow balcony, which we were allowed to use, sentinels, however, being stationed on it. When I looked out in the morning, I could not help being struck by an odd, and not pleasant coincidence. On that day, forty-seven years before, my grand-father, Mr. F. S. Key, then a prisoner on a British ship, had witnessed the bombardment of Fort McHenry. When, on the following morning, the hostile fleet drew off, defeated, he wrote the song so long popular throughout the country, "Star Spangled Banner." As I stood upon the very scene of that conflict, I could not but contrast my position with his, forty-seven years before. The flag which he had then so proudly hailed, I saw waving, at the same place, over the victims of as vulgar and brutal a despotism as modern times have witnessed.

At an early hour in the morning, and through the day, a number of our friends endeavored to procure access to us, but nearly all failed to do so. Three or four gentlemen and two or three ladies managed to obtain admission to the Fort, and Col. Morris, the commanding officer, permitted them to interchange a few words with us, in his presence, they being down on the parade-ground and we up in the balcony. Mr. Brown was not even allowed to speak to his wife, who had been suffered to enter the Fort, and could only take leave of her by bowing to her across the parade ground.

About mid-day, we sent for our clothes, several of the party having left home without bringing anything whatever with them. At 4 o'clock, P. M., we were notified that we were to be sent at 5 o'clock to Fortress Monroe. The trunks of most of us fortunately arrived half an hour before we left, and were thoroughly searched. Had they been delayed a little longer we should undoubtedly have been sent off with only such little clothing as some of us happened to have brought with us when first arrested. As it was, one or two of the party had absolutely nothing save what they wore. About 6 o'clock we left Fort McHenry on the steamer Adelaide. The after-cabin, which was very comfortable, and the after-deck, on which it opened, were assigned to our use. Sentinels were stationed in the cabin and on the after-deck. The officers and crew of the boat treated us with all the kindness and courtesy it was in their power to show. When we were taken below to supper, we saw at another table a number of naval officers, some of whom several of my companions had known well. These officers did not venture to recognize a single individual of our party, although we were within ten feet of them, and within full view. Their conduct was in admirable keeping with that of the Government they served.

Fortress Monroe.

WE reached Fortress Monroe about 6 o'clock, on the morning of September 14th. Major-General JOHN E. WOOL was in command of the Department within which the Fort was situated, and had his headquarters there at the time.— As no arrangements had been made for our reception, we did not land until late in the day. The boat lay at the wharf for several hours, and then ran up above the Fortress about a quarter of a mile, and anchored in the stream. In the course of the day General WOOL sent for Messrs. BROWN and MAY. He stated to them that our arrival had taken him by surprise, and that he had no quarters prepared for us, but said that some of the casemates were being made ready for us. He evidently felt that the accommodations he was about to give us were not such as we had a right to expect, and intimated that a building known as Carroll Hall, or a portion of it, would, in all probability, be assigned to us in a few days. This was the last that any of the party saw of General WOOL, and we heard no more of Carroll Hall. About 5 o'clock we landed, and were marched to our quarters. These consisted of two casemates, from which some negroes were still engaged in removing dirt and rubbish, when we got there. Each of these casemates was divided by a substantial partition, thus making four rooms. The two front rooms were well finished, and were about fifteen by twenty-three feet each, and each had a door and two windows which opened on the grounds within the Fortress. The windows had Venetian shutters to them, and there were Venetian doors also, outside of the ordinary solid doors. The inner, or back rooms, if rooms they can be called, were considerably smaller than the others, and were simply vaulted chambers of rough stone, whitewashed. — They were each lighted by a single, deep embrasure, which, at the narrowest part, was about forty-four by twenty-two inches. Just beneath these embrasures was the moat, which at that point was more than fifty feet in width. On the opposite side of the moat a sentinel was constantly stationed. The two back rooms and one of the front ones we used as sleeping apartments, each being occupied by five persons. — In the other front room we took our meals. Bedsteads and bedding were furnished us, which, I believe, were obtained from the Hygeia Hotel, just outside the walls. About 10 o'clock one of the Sergeants of the Provost Marshal visited us, and carefully searched our baggage. Our meals were sent from the Hotel also, and worse, as we at that time thought, could not well have been offered us. The regulations to which we were subjected, were not only unnecessarily rigorous, but seemed to have been framed with the deliberate purpose of adding petty insults to our other annoyances. We were required to leave the room when the servants who brought our meals were engaged in setting the table, although a Sergeant of the Guard was always present at such times, to prevent our holding any conversation with them. We were notified, by an order from General WOOL also, that the knives and forks were to be counted after each meal. It is difficult to conceive for what rational purpose such a rule was made. Fifteen of us would scarcely have thought of assailing the thousands of troops who composed the garrison, with such weapons as might have been snatched from the table; and, closely guarded as we were, it was hardly possible that we could have effected our escape, had we thought of doing so, by means of such implements as knives and forks. The order was one, therefore, which could only have been intended to humiliate us, and it was certainly such as no one having the instincts of a gentleman, or the better feelings of a man, would have suggested or enforced. It was, however, in accordance with the theory upon which General WOOL thought proper to deal with us throughout.

In front of our casemates a large guard was stationed day and night, two or three tents being pitched about ten feet off for their use; and a sentinel was constantly pacing up and down within four feet of our doors. For a week we never left our two casemates for a single instant, for any purpose whatever. We continually remonstrated against the manner in which we were treated, and represented the fact that we were likely, under such circumstances, to suffer seriously in health. Our complaints were generally followed by some new restriction. After we had been there two or three days, the Sergeant of the Guard closed the window-shutters and the Venetian doors of our rooms, and stated that he had express orders to do so. At our request, Mr. WALLIS addressed the following note to Capt. DAVIS, the Provost Marshal:

"CAPT. DAVIS, U. S. A.,

Provost Marshal:

"SIR : The Sergeant who has charge of my fellow prisoners and myself, has just closed the blinds of our front windows and doors, excluding us from the sight of passing objects, shutting out, to a great extent, the light by which we read, and hindering the circulation of the air through our apartments. These last are, at best, damp and unwholesome, and to-day particularly, in the existing state of the atmosphere, are extremely unpleasant and uncomfortable—so much so, that we have been compelled to build a fire for our mere protection from illness. Some of our number are old men ; others in delicate health ; and the restraint which excludes us from air and exercise is painful enough without this new annoyance, which the Sergeant informs us he has no right to forego. You are aware of the disgusting necessities to which we are subjected, in a particular of which we spoke to you personally, and you will, of course, know how much this new obstruction must add to our discomfort. I am requested by my companions simply to call your attention to the matter, and am,   Very respectfully,

"S. T. WALLIS.

"FORTRESS MONROE, 17*th Sept.*, 1861."

No reply was made to this by Capt. DAVIS. On the following day iron bars were placed across the shutters and padlocked, thus fastening them permanently, and the Venetian doors were padlocked also. The keys were kept by the Sergeant, who was the deputy, or assistant, of the Provost Marshal, and, in his absence, no one had access to our rooms. In consequence of this, we were often put to serious inconvenience, and on several occasions, our meals, which were trundled up from the hotel on a wheelbarrow, remained for an hour or two outside of the door, awaiting the pleasure of the Sergeant. After the closing of the doors and shutters, our situation was of course, far more irksome than ever.— The Venetian doors were not quite so high as the solid doors, and by standing on anything that elevated us a few inches, we could manage to look out over them. Through these furtive and unsatisfactory glimpses only, could we obtain any sight of the outer world on that side of our prison. From the back rooms we had a limited view of the river, and of some of the shipping; and of this prospect it was impossible by the exercise of any ingenuity to deprive us.— A day or two before we left, we were allowed, at intervals during the day, the use of an adjoining casemate. Sanitary considerations, I presume, compelled our keepers to grant us a privilege, which it was sheer brutality to have so long denied us. A door communicated between our quarters and this new casemate, at which a sentinel was stationed, who permitted two persons to pass at one time. The more disgusting and painful details of our imprisonment, I must abstain from dwelling on. Our rooms were swept each morning, and such other personal services as were absolutely necessary, were hurriedly performed by two filthy negro boys, under the supervision of the Sergeant of the Guard.

We were permitted to correspond with our families and friends, all our letters undergoing the scrutiny of one of General WOOL's officers. But we were not allowed to make any public statements, nor even to correct the falsehoods or slanders which were circulated about us in the newspapers. On one occasion, a paragraph appeared in the Baltimore *American*, which by way of justifying our arrest, alleged that the Government had in its possession

ample evidence of the fact, that all who had been arrested
had in some way violated the laws. An assertion so utterly
false we naturally desired to contradict, and Messrs. BROWN,
and WALLIS, and myself, each wrote a brief card for publi-
cation in other journals, denying the truth of the *American's*
statement. These cards were not allowed to go to the
newspapers to which we had addressed them. It apparently
suited the purpose of the Government to have us libelled as
well as punished, and we, of course, were without redress.

For ten days we lived as I have described, in these dark-
ened and dreary casemates. General WOOL never came
near our quarters, nor did he ever, either directly or
indirectly, extend to us the slightest courtesy. He knew as
well as any one, that we had been seized and were held by
the Government in utter violation of all law, and that he
had no decent pretext for permitting himself to be made our
custodian. He knew therefore that we were entitled to be
treated with some consideration. But he ignored, alike,
his obligations as a citizen and as a gentleman, and caused
us to be subjected to indignities that it would have been
needless to inflict on the convicted inmates of his own
guard-house. After our return, we heard in several
quarters, that General WOOL had repeatedly said he
acted in the matter, strictly in accordance with his instructions from Washington. As implicit deference to officers of
the Government seems to be generally exacted in these
days, the public may perhaps accept General WOOL's
explanation. For myself, I do not; and I am sure there
are many who will refuse to credit the statement that the
War Department found time at such a crisis, to send
special orders to Fortress Monroe, consigning us to the
casemates in question, and directing the closing of the
shutters, and the counting of the knives and forks. It
seems more reasonable to suppose that General WOOL had
some discretionary powers in regard to the treatment he
was to accord to his prisoners.

Soon after we reached Fortress Monroe, we began to
consider the probabilities of our release, and the means by
which we might obtain it. It was suggested that we
3

should come to some understanding as to the course we
ought to pursue, and then act together throughout; but this
proposition was not for a moment entertained. Almost
every one of us thought that each individual should act
for himself, under his own sense of right. It was very
soon evident however, that we were all of one opinion.
We regarded the outrage done us personally, as one about
which we could make no compromise.. We thought the
contemptuous violation of the laws of our State and the
rights of its people, required at our hands all the resistance
we could offer. We saw that Mr. LINCOLN desired, by
arbitrary measures, to silence everything like opposition to
his schemes, and we felt under an obligation to thwart his
iniquitous project, by showing that the people of Maryland
could not successfully be so dealt with. It seemed clear to
us, therefore, that it was the duty of each of us, both as
an individual and a citizen, to continue to denounce and
protest against Mr. LINCOLN's proceedings, and to accept at
his hands, nothing save the unconditional discharge, to
which we were entitled. Of this determination, we notified
our friends during the first few days of our imprisonment.

Fort La Fayette.

On the afternoon of the 25th of September, we left Fortress Monroe, on the steamer George Peabody. There were no other passengers, but the fifteen or twenty soldiers composing the guard. The boat was a Baltimore boat, and we received from her officers and crew the same courteous treatment that had been extended to us on board of the Adelaide. We reached Fort La Fayette, in New York harbor, a little before dark, on the afternoon of the 26th, and were immediately transferred from the boat to the Fort. Fort La Fayette is built upon a shoal, or small island, lying in the Narrows, just between the lower end of Staten Island and Long Island, and two or three hundred yards from the latter. It is something of an octagonal structure, though the four principal sides are so much longer than the others, that the building, on the inside, looks like a square. It is some forty-five or fifty feet high. In two of the longer and two of the shorter sides, which command the channel, are the batteries. There are two tiers of heavy guns on each of these sides, and above these, are lighter *barbette* guns under a temporary wooden roof. The other two principal sides are occupied, on the first and second stories, by small casemates ; all those on the second and some of those on the first story, being then assigned to the officers and soldiers. There are, altogether, ten of these casemates on each story. The whole space enclosed within the walls is about one hundred and twenty feet across. A pavement about twenty-five feet wide runs around this space, leaving a patch of ground some seventy feet square, in the middle. A gloomier looking place than Fort La Fayette, both within and without, it would be hard to find in the whole State of New York, or, indeed, anywhere. On the high bluff on Long Island stood Fort Hamilton, an extensive fortification, whose commanding officer, Col. MARTIN BURKE, had also jurisdiction over Fort La Fayette. Lieut. CHAS. O. WOOD, who had a few months before received a commission from Mr. LINCOLN, was commanding officer at Fort La Fayette. The two principal gun batteries, and four of the casemates in the lower story, were assigned to the prisoners. Each of these batteries was paved with brick, and was, I should judge, about sixty feet long and twenty-four feet wide. The one in which I was first quartered was lighted by five embrasures, the breadth and height of each being about two-and-a-half by two feet, and on the outside of these, iron gratings had been fastened. There were five large thirty-two pounders in this room, which were about eight feet apart, and with their carriages occupied a great deal of space. Five large doorways, seven or eight feet high, opened upon the enclosure within the walls, and were closed by solid folding doors. We were only allowed to keep two of these doors, at one end of the battery, open, and at that end only could we usually see to read or write. The lower half of the battery was in a state of perpetual twilight. The adjoining battery was in all respects like the one I have attempted to describe. The four casemates which were occupied by prisoners, were vaulted cells, measuring twenty-four by fourteen feet in length and breadth; and eight feet at the highest point. Each was lighted by two small loop holes in the outer wall, about ten inches · wide, and by a similar one opening on the inside enclosure. These casemates were both dark and damp, but they had fire-places in them, while it was impossible to warm the gun batteries, until stoves were put up about a week or ten days before we left.

The Fort could not be made to accommodate twenty people decently besides the garrison. Nevertheless, there were always largely over a hundred crowded into it, and at one time there were as many as one hundred and thirty-five.

When I and my companions reached the wharf, we were met by Lieut. Wood. I had seen him at Fort Hamilton some six weeks before, having gone there to try and see my father, who was then confined in Fort La Fayette. Wood recognized me, and requested me to introduce to him the gentlemen who were with me. This was the first and last occasion, as far as I know, on which he manifested a disposition to treat us with civility. His bearing at all times subsequently, was that of an ordinary jailor, except, perhaps, that he displayed even less good feeling than usually characterizes that class of people. We were marched into the gun battery I have mentioned, and as the prisoners already there, many of whom were our acquaintances or friends, crowded around us, Lieutenant Wood requested all to leave the room, except those comprised in what he elegantly termed the "last lot." We were then required to give up all the money in our possession. We were each furnished that night with an iron bedstead, a bag of straw, and one shoddy blanket. When we had time to look around us, we found there were some twenty prisoners already quartered in the battery, and the number of inmates was therefore increased to about thirty-five by the addition of our party. The beds, which were arranged between the guns, almost touched each other. If we had had other furniture, we should not have known what to do with it, three or four chairs and a couple of small tables being all that we could afterwards find space for.

We found in the morning that the gun battery adjoining ours was, if possible, more crowded than the one we occupied, and the casemates were as much crowded as the batteries. There were as I have stated, four casemates on the lower or ground floor, allotted to prisoners. Three of these contained nine or ten persons each, and into the fourth were thrust at that time very nearly thirty prisoners, who were either privateersmen, or sailors who had been taken while running the blockade on the Southern coast. These men had neither beds nor blankets, and were all, or nearly all, in irons. Their situation was wretched in the extreme.

Such was the condition of things at Fort La Fayette when we reached it, and we were not a little astonished to learn from our friends, who had been there longer, that their situation had been even worse a few weeks previously, than it then was. To give a correct idea of the manner in which the Government dealt with gentlemen who, by its own admission, had been arrested, or were then held merely by way of precaution, I insert the following letters, which had, before my arrival, been sent by my father to the parties to whom they are respectively addressed :

"Fort La Fayette, N. Y., *August 1st*, 1861.

"Hon SIMON CAMERON, *Sec'y of War*,

"Washington, D. C.

"Sir :

"After the interview I had with you in Fort McHenry on the 4th ulto., and in view of the assurances you then expressed, as to the manner in which I and the gentlemen with me, were entitled to be treated during our confinement by the General Government, I cannot refrain from expressing my surprise, at the condition in which, by its orders, we now find ourselves. On Monday evening last, we were placed on board the steamer Joseph Whitney, with a detachment of soldiers ; all information as to our place of destination, being positively refused, both to us and to the members of our families. Both General Dix and Major Morris, however, gave the most positive assurances that, at the place to which we should be taken, we would be made much more comfortable, and the limits of our confinement would be less restricted than at Fort McHenry. Yesterday we were landed here, and are kept in close custody. No provision whatever had been made here for us, and last night we were shut up, eight persons in a vaulted room or casemate, about twenty-four by fourteen feet, having three small windows, each about three feet by fourteen inches, and a close wooden door, which was shut and locked upon us soon after 9 o'clock, and remained so until morning. Some of the party, by permission, brought on our own bedsteads and bedding with which we had been compelled to supply ourselves at Fort McHenry; otherwise we should have been compelled to lie on the bare floor, the officers here stating to us, that they had no supplies whatever, and could not furnish us with blankets, even of the most ordinary kind. We are distinctly notified that the orders under which the commanding officer of the post is acting, require him to impose upon us the following, among other restrictions, viz. : we are allowed to receive or forward no letters from or to, even our own families, unless they are submitted to inspection and perusal by some military officer;—no friend can visit us without the permission of Colonel Burke, whose quarters are not at this Fort, and no intimation has been given that such permission will be readily granted ;—we are to receive no newspapers from any quarter ;—for one hour in the morning, and one in the evening only, we are to be allowed to take exercise by walking about in a small square, not larger than some sixty or seventy feet each way, surrounded on the four sides by the massive buildings of the Fort, three stories in height. We were, on our arrival here, required to surrender all the money we had, and all writing paper and envelopes—our baggage being all searched for these and other articles that might be chosen to be considered as contraband. It is unnecessary to give any further details to satisfy you, that our condition, as to physical comfort, is no better than that of the worst felons in any common jail in the country. Having been arrested and already imprisoned for a month, without a charge of any legal offence having been, as yet, preferred against me, or those arrested at the same time with me, it is useless to make any further protest to you against the continuance of our confinement.— But we do insist, as a matter of common right, as well as in fulfilment of your own declarations to me, that if the government chooses to exercise its power, by restraining us of our liberty, it is bound in ordinary decency to make such provision for our comfort and health, as gentlemen against whom, if charges have been preferred, they have not been made known, and all opportunity for an investigation has been denied, are recognized in every civilized community to be entitled to. It is but just to Colonel Burke and Lieutenant Wood, who commands the garrison here, that I should add, that both of those officers have professed their desire to extend to us all comforts, that their instructions will allow, and the means at their command will enable them to do. They have, however, each stated that the orders under which they act, are imperative, and that their supplies of even the most common articles, are at present very limited. I have written this letter on my bed, sitting on the floor, upon a carpet bag, there being neither table, chair, stool or bench in the room.

"I have the honor to be

"Your obedient servant,

"CHARLES HOWARD."

"Fort La Fayette, N. Y. Harbor, *August 7th*, 1861.

"Hon. SIMON CAMERON, *Sec'ry of War*,

"Washington, D. C.

"Sir :—

"I addressed a communication yesterday to Colonel Burke, which he advised me he has forwarded to Washington. In reply, he has written a note to Lieutenant Wood, and instructed him to read it to us. The substance of this note was, that as some of the letters we had written to our families, if they were to find their way into the newspapers, 'might influence the public mind,' the Colonel had thought it proper to forward them all to the headquarters of the army. He further stated that the orders he had received were, to 'treat us kindly, but keep us safely.' As to the first part, allow me to say, that whatever our condition may be, the minds of our friends, and of all others, who may feel any interest in the matter, will surely be less apt to be influenced unfavorably towards the government by knowing the truth about us, than they will be by their finding that our communications with them are intercepted, and that they are allowed to hear nothing whatever as to how we are treated. They will necessarily conclude that our imprisonment is exactly like that of those who used to be confined in the Bastile, (as in fact it is,) who were allowed to hold no communications except such as might be entirely agreeable and acceptable to their custodians. They will, of course, be kept in a continual state of great anxiety and uneasiness, and their sympathies will be constantly excited in our behalf. The distress that will thus be inflicted upon our families, can be termed nothing less than cruelty. In the next place, it is hard to conceive how it can be reconciled, with anything like the idea of 'kind treatment,' to prohibit our reception of all newspapers whatever, or the unrestricted delivery to us, without examination, of all letters that may be addressed to us; whilst it certainly cannot be shown that such prohibitions are at all necessary to ensure our 'safe-keeping.' The examination of, and the discretion claimed to retain letters to us from the nearest members of our families, as well as the preventing us from receiving newspapers, can only be regarded as measures of punishment, adopted towards those who have been convicted of no offence; to whom no opportunity has been afforded for an investigation of any charges that may possibly have been preferred against them; and for whose arrest, as our counsel were assured by General BANKS, there were no other reasons than the allegations set forth by him in his proclamation; and the continuance of whose confinement, he stated to be solely a precautionary measure on the part of the government. These assurances were given by him at Fort McHenry. I will add that, whatever may be the disposition of the officer commanding the post, and of those in this garrison, to 'treat us kindly,' they are restricted in doing so, within extremely narrow limits, either by other orders they may have received, or by the means of extending such treatment not having been supplied to them. We are isolated—at a distance of two hundred miles from our families, and all but a few friends; and with these we are permitted to have no intercourse. We are thrown upon our own resources—those of us who may have means, being allowed to find, at our own cost, within the Fort, decent, but very ordinary fare, whilst those who cannot, in justice to their families, afford such expense, have nothing but the ordinary rations of the soldier, which are of the coarsest kind. In consequence of the delay in other departments of the service, in complying with the requisitions which the officers here have made, we should at this moment, though we have been here a week, have been without a chair or table but for the courtesy of Lieutenant STIRLING, who, seeing our state of utter discomfort, has lent to us two chairs from his own quarters; and that of the wife of a Sergeant, who has lent us a small stand. We are informed, however, that a supply of such articles may be expected, for our use, from the city, this evening. Finally, there are six of us confined in one room, precisely similar, in all respects, to that described in my letter of the 1st inst., to which I beg leave to refer you.

   "I have the honor to be

    "Your obedient servant,

      "CHARLES HOWARD."

"Fort La Fayette, N. Y. Harbor, *August 8th*, 1861.

"Lieut. Gen. SCOTT, *Commander-in-Chief, U. S. A.*

"Headquarters, Washington, D. C.

"Sir:

"By a letter received last night from Mrs. Howard, I learn that in reply to the inquiries she made of you, she was informed that I would be "decently lodged and subsisted here." I wrote to the Hon. the Secretary of War, on the 1st inst., and again yesterday, advising him of the treatment which I and my fellow prisoners are receiving. A perusal of those letters would satisfy you that these assurances are not verified. I need here only say, that we are not "decently lodged," nor are we in any sense of the words "decently subsisted" by the Government. The only proffer of subsistence made to us, has been to feed us like the private soldiers of the garrison, or to allow us to procure other meals at our own cost.

"I have the honor to be

"Your obedient servant,

"CHARLES HOWARD."

"Fort La Fayette, N. Y. Harbor, *August 12th*, 1861.

"Hon. SIMON CAMERON, *Sec'y of War,*

"Washington, D. C.

"Sir:

"I laid before you a statement of the condition in which I am kept, in two former communications, the one on the 1st inst., and the other a few days subsequently; to which I beg leave to refer. And I should not again trouble you, had I not, since my last, learned on the direct authority of Lieutenant-General Scott, that an order had been given by the Department of State, that the political prisoners confined at Fort La Fayette, shall be "decently lodged and subsisted, unless they prefer to provide for themselves." The "decent lodging" furnished us, consists in putting seven gentlemen to sleep in one room, of which I have before given you a description. Within this or at the door of it, we are required to remain, except during two hours in the day or whilst taking our meals.

The "decent subsistence" offered us, in the alternative of our declining, or not having the means to provide for ourselves, is much inferior in many respects, to that furnished to convicted felons in the Baltimore Penitentiary and Jail; and so far as I am informed, in any well-regulated prison in the country.

"The officers here advise us, that this is the only fare which, under the instructions given, and the means allowed to them by the Government, they can offer. How far such treatment is in accordance with the instructions of the Government, as expressed by the Department of State, with the assurance given to me personally by yourself, or with the promises voluntarily made by Major-General JOHN A. DIX, and Major WM. W. MORRIS, I leave it, sir, for you to judge.

"I have the honor to be

"Your obedient servant,

"CHARLES HOWARD."

"FORT LA FAYETTE, N. Y. Harbor, *August* 19th, 1861.

"HON. WM. H. SEWARD, *Sec'y of State,*

WASHINGTON, D. C.

"SIR:

"My family were informed by Lieutenant-General SCOTT, under date of the 3d inst., that an order had been given 'by the Department of State, that the political prisoners confined at Fort La Fayette shall be decently lodged and subsisted, unless they prefer to provide for themselves.' About the same time I was advised by Lieutenant-Colonel BURKE, commanding this post, that his instructions were 'to treat us kindly, but keep us safely.' I beg leave, sir, to inform you that your order has not been complied with. It cannot be considered as 'decent lodging' to put a number of gentlemen accustomed to the comforts of life, to sleep in one low vaulted room, in or at the door of which they are confined, except for two hours in the twenty-four. The number sleeping in the room in which I am now placed, has varied from five to seven. There are now here, six of us. The only subsistence provided for us by the Government, as the alternative of providing for ourselves, has been the proffer of the single ration, distributed here to the private soldier, which is inferior both in quantity and quality, to the fare furnished to the convicted felons in many of the jails and penitentiaries throughout the country. And this is the 'decent subsistence,' offered to men who have been arrested, and are held on suspicion only, and who have not ceased to demand an open investigation of any charges that may possibly have been preferred against them; a demand which has been persistently denied. I have no grounds for imputing to Colonel BURKE, or the officers of this garrison, any intentional disposition to treat us unkindly. But acting as they state themselves to be, in obedience to the orders which they have received, we are subject to various harsh and arbitrary restrictions, which are utterly irreconcilable with the idea of 'kind treatment,' whilst they are equally unnecessary for the ensuring of our safe-keeping. I deem it useless at present, to go more into details, as I have already described the condition in which we are placed, in three communications to the Hon. the Secretary of War, on the 1st, 7th and 12th inst. respectively, and in one to Lieutenant-General SCOTT, on the 8th inst., of none of which does any notice appear to have been taken. Should you, sir, however, desire a fuller statement than I have here made, to be addressed directly to yourself, one shall be forwarded, as soon as I may be apprised of your wishes.

" I have the honor to be

" Your obedient servant,

"CHARLES HOWARD."

Not the slightest notice was taken of these letters by the persons to whom they were addressed, unless the few chairs, and sheets, and blankets, which were furnished some time afterwards, were distributed by special order from Washington.

To show how desirous the officers of the Government were, at that time, to keep, even from the families of the prisoners, all knowledge of their actual condition, I am permitted to cite this letter from Mr. GATCHELL, one of the Police Commissioners of Baltimore. Lieutenant WOOD refused to forward it to its destination. It was written in pencil:

"FORT LA FAYETTE, New York.

"MY DEAR WIFE:—

"I write on my knee, and with very little light—but I cannot help saying to you, so that you may know as soon as possible, that, notwithstanding the assurances given to us when we left Fort McHenry, we are altogether as uncomfortable as it is possible to be. The gentleman in command has expressed his desire to do all in his power for our comfort, but he has not the means. Don't write until I give you notice, for at present we are cut off from all communication with our friends, except writing to them, and our letters inspected. Love to all.   Affectionately,

"WM. H. GATCHELL.

"*Wednesday Evening, 31st July.*"

Lieutenant WOOD, who had expressed his desire to do all in his power for the comfort of the prisoners, sent back the above letter after the lapse of two or three weeks, to Mr. GATCHELL. He informed Mr. GATCHELL, when he returned it, that it had been forwarded to Washington for inspection, and that he was not allowed to let it pass.

I had, during the visit to New York, of which I have already spoken, learned how outrageously my father and his companions were treated, and I published in the New York *Daily News*, a full statement of the facts. It was never contradicted by the agents of the Government, and was apparently unnoticed by the public. At that time, also, I met Major CLITZ, of the United States Army, who was then stationed at Fort Hamilton, who, in reply to some remarks of mine, admitted that there were not decent accommodations in Fort La Fayette for fifteen prisoners. Major CLITZ came over to Fort La Fayette while I was myself a prisoner there, and I reminded him of that conversation. He unhesitatingly replied that he was still of the same opinion.

Shortly after the visit just mentioned, the prisoners were permitted to receive the daily papers, and were allowed the use of liquor, under certain restrictions. The liquor they chose to order, were kept by Lieut. WOOD, and were given out, day by day, in moderate quantities. The day after we arrived, we sent to New York for beds, bedding and other necessary articles of furniture. These we received a few days arterwards. Before our arrival, those of the prisoners who chose to do so, had obtained permission to board with the Ordnance Sergeant, who had been many years at the post. He and his family occupied two or three of the lower casemates, and he undertook to furnish us two meals daily at a charge, to each prisoner, of a dollar a day. This arrangement most of our party adopted. The others preferred or could not afford to do otherwise than accept the Government rations, upon which the majority of the prisoners were living. These were of the coarsest description, and were served in the coarsest style. A tin plate and a tin cup to each person constituted the whole table furniture. The dinners consisted of fat pork and beans, a cup of thin soup and bread, or of boiled beef and potatoes and bread on alternate days. For breakfast, bread, and weak, unpalatable coffee, were distributed. This fare was precisely the same as that furnished to the soldiers. I more than once examined these rations after they were served. The coffee was a muddy liquid in which the taste of coffee was barely perceptible, the predominating flavor being a combination of burnt beans and foul water. The soup was, if possible, worse, the only palatable thing about it being the few stray grains of rice that could sometimes be fished out of each can. The pork and beef were of the most indifferent quality, and were at times only half cooked. Over and over again have I seen gentlemen who had been always accustomed to all the comforts of life, forced to turn away with loathing from the miserable food thus provided for them. The fare furnished to those of us who boarded with the Sergeant, was very plain, but good enough of its kind.

On the 8th of October we addressed the following remonstrance to the President. The statements which it contains, were purposely made as moderate and temperate as was consistent with the truth.

"FORT LA FAYETTE, 8th October, 1861.

"*His Excellency, the President of the United States,*

"SIR:

"The undersigned, prisoners confined in Fort La Fayette, are compelled to address this protest and remonstrance against the inhumanity of their confinement and treatment. The officers in command at Fort Hamilton and this post, being fully aware of the grievances and privations to which we are obliged to submit, we are bound for humanity's sake, to presume that they have no authority or means to redress or remove them. They in fact, assure us that they have not. Our only recourse therefore, is to lay this statement before you, in order that you may interpose to prevent our being any longer exposed to them.

"The prisoners at this post are confined in four small casemates, and two large battery-rooms. The former are about fourteen feet in breadth by twenty-four or thereabouts in length, with arched ceilings about eight-and-a-half feet high at the highest point, the spring of the arch commencing at about five feet from the floor. In each of these is a fire-place, and the floors are of plank. The battery-rooms are of considerably higher pitch, and the floors are of brick, and a large space is occupied in them by the heavy guns and gun-carriages of the batteries. They have no fire-places or means of protection from cold or moisture, and the doors are large, like those of a carriage-house, rendering the admission of light impossible without entire exposure to the temperature and weather without. In one of the small casemates, twenty-three prisoners are confined, two-thirds of them in irons, without beds, bedding, or any of the commonest necessaries. Their condition could hardly be worse, if they were in a slave-ship, on the middle passage. In each of two, out of the three other casemates, ten gentlemen are imprisoned; in the third there are nine, and a tenth is allotted to it; their beds and necessary luggage leaving them scarce space to move, and rendering the commonest personal cleanliness almost an impossibility. The doors are all fastened from six or thereabouts in the evening, until the same hour in the morning, and with all the windows (which are small) left open in all weathers, it is hardly possible to sleep in the foul, unwholesome air. Into one of the larger battery-rooms, there are thirty-four prisoners closely crowded; into the other, thirty-five. All the doors are closed for the same period as stated above, and the only ventilation is then from the embrasures, and so imperfect that the atmosphere is oppressive and almost stifling. Even during the day, three of the doors of one of these apartments are kept closed, against the remonstrances of the medical men who are among the inmates, and to the utter exclusion of wholesome and necessary light and air. In damp weather, all these unhealthy annoyances and painful discomforts are of course greatly augmented, and when, as to-day, the prisoners are compelled by rain to continue within doors, their situation becomes almost intolerable. The undersigned do not hesitate to say, that no intelligent inspector of prisons can fail to pronounce their accommodations as wretchedly deficient, and altogether incompatible with health, and it is obvious, as we already feel, that the growing inclemencies of the season which is upon us, must make our condition more and more nearly unendurable. Many of the prisoners are men advanced in life; many more are of infirm health or delicate constitutions. The greater portion of them have been accustomed to the reasonable comforts of life, none of which are accessible to them here, and their liability to illness, is, of course, proportionately greater on that account. Many have already suffered seriously, from indisposition augmented by the restrictions imposed upon them. A contagious cutaneous disease is now spreading in one of the larger apartments, and the physicians who are among us, are positive that some serious general disorder must be the inevitable result, if our situation remains unimproved. The use of any but salt water, except for drinking, has been, for some time, altogether denied to us. The cistern water, itself, for some days past, has been filled with dirt and animalcules, and the supply, even of that, has been so low, that yesterday we were almost wholly without drinking-water. A few of us, who have the means to purchase some trifling necessaries, have been able to relieve ourselves from this latter privation, to some extent, by procuring an occasional, though greatly inadequate, supply of fresh water from the Long Island side.

It only remains to add, that the fare is of the commonest and coarsest soldiers' rations, almost invariably ill-prepared and ill-cooked. Some of us, who are better able than the rest, are permitted to take our meals at a private mess, supplied by the wife of the Ordnance Sergeant, for which we pay, at the rate of a dollar per day, from our own funds. Those who are less fortunate, are compelled to submit to a diet so bad and unusual, as to be seriously prejudicial to their health.

The undersigned have entered into these partial details, because they cannot believe that it is the purpose of the government to destroy their health or sacrifice their lives, by visiting them with such cruel hardships, and they will hope, unless forced to a contrary conclusion, that it can only be necessary to present the facts to you, plainly, in order to secure the necessary relief. We desire to say nothing, here, in regard to the justice or injustice of our imprisonment, but we respectfully insist upon our right to be treated with decency and common humanity, so long as the government sees fit to confine us.

"Commending the matter to your earliest consideration and prompt interference, we are your obedient servants,

H. MAY,
E. C. LOWBER,
WM. G. HARRISON,
ROBT. MURE,
JNO. WILLIAMS,
ROBT. M. DENISON,
SAML. H. LYON,
L. SANGSTON,
G. O. VAN AMRINGE,
HILARY CENAS,
W. R. BUTT,
B. P. LOYALL,
W. H. WARD,
T. PARKIN SCOTT,
P. F. RAISIN,
JNO. C. BRAINE,
J. H. GORDON,
C. J. DURANT,
M. W. BARR,
R. T. DURRETT,
J. HANSON THOMAS,
C. J. FAULKNER,
CHAS. HOWARD,
GEO. WM. BROWN,
WM. H. GATCHELL,
C. S. MOREHEAD,
JAS. A. MCMASTER,
CHAS. H. PITTS,
R. H. ALVEY,
S. T. WALLIS,
AUSTIN E. SMITH,
F. K. HOWARD,

J. T. MCFEAT,
J. K. MILLNER,
B. MILLS, M. D.,
ANDREW LYNCH, M. D.
H. R. STEVENS,
J. W. ROBARTS,
R. R. WALKER,
CHAS. M. HAGELIN,
BETHEL BURTON,
S. J. ANDERSON,
RICH. S. FREEMAN,
G. P. PRESSAY,
L. G. QUINLAN,
W. E. KEARNEY,
G. A. SHACKLEFORD,
JNO. H. CUSICK,
JOS. W. GRIFFITH,
ROBT. DRANE,
JNO. W. DAVIS,
T. S. WILSON,
ROBT. TANSILL,
A. D. WHARTON,
SAML. EAKINS,
J. B. BARBOUR,
EDW. PAYNE,
A. DAWSON,
JNO. M. BREWER,
ELLIS B. SCHNABEL,
H. B. CLAIBORNE,
F. WYATT,
E. S. RUGGLES,
JAS. E. MURPHRY,

5

HENRY M. WARFIELD,	L. S. HOBSCLAW,
GEO. P. KANE,	ALGERNON S. SULLIVAN,
CHAS. MACGILL, M. D.,	JAS. CHAPIN,
GEO. W. BARNARD,	E. B. WILDER,
F. M. CROW,	A. McDOWELL,
H. G. THURBER,	WM. GRUBBS,
E. G. KILBOURNE,	CHAS. KOPPERL,
T. H. WOOLDRIDGE,	THOS. W. HALL, Jr.

On the 10th of October, the following note was sent to Lieutenant WOOD, who ordered it to be read to the prisoners:

"FORT HAMILTON, New York, *October* 10*th*, 1861.

"SIR:—

"I am directed by Colonel BURKE to say to you, that you can inform the prisoners, that their Petition has been forwarded, through Colonel TOWNSEND, to the President United States.

"Very respectfully,

"Your obedient servant,

"J. C. LAY,

"*First Lieutenant 12th Infantry.*

"P.S.—Colonel presumed that boat has brought you a supply of water.   J. C. L."

Of the gentlemen who signed the above remonstrance, which Colonel BURKE thought proper to term a "Petition," many were members of the Maryland Legislature; a large number were, up to the time of their incarceration, officers of the Navy; and others were men of high social or political position in their respective States. No reply was ever received from Washington.

The rules to which we were expected to conform, were posted on the walls of the different batteries and casemates. They read as follows:

"REGULATIONS FOR THE GUIDANCE OF CITIZEN PRISONERS
CONFINED AT THIS POST.

"1*st*.—The rooms of the prisoners will be ready for inspection at 9 o'clock, A.M. All cleaning, &c., will be done by the prisoners themselves, unless otherwise directed. All washing will be done in the yard.

"2*d*.—No conversation will be allowed with any member of this garrison, and all communication in regard to their wants will be made to the Sergeant of the Guard.

"3*d*.—No prisoner will leave his room without the permission of the Sergeant of the Guard. * * * * * * * * *

"4*th*.—Prisoners will avoid all conversations on the political affairs of this country, within the hearing of any member of this garrison.

"5*th*.—Light will be allowed in the prisoners' rooms until 9.15, P.M. After this hour, all talking, or noise of any kind, will cease.

"6*th*.—The prisoners will obey implicitly the directions of any member of the guard.

"7*th*.—Cases of sickness will be reported at 7, A.M.

"8*th*.—Any transgressions of the foregoing rules will be corrected by solitary imprisonment, or such other restrictions as may be required to the strict enforcement thereof.

[Signed]   "CHARLES O. WOOD,
                    "*Second Lieutenant, 9th Infantry*,
                              "Commanding Post.

"FORT LA FAYETTE, *New York Harbor*, August 3d, 1861."

Shortly after we arrived at Fort La Fayette, the following additional order was issued:

"No prisoners will be allowed to recognize or have any communication with any persons visiting this Fort, excepting when the visitor brings an order from the proper authority, permitting an interview, which interview will be held in the presence of an officer, and not to exceed one hour; the conversation during the interview will be carried on in a tone of voice loud enough to be distinctly heard by the officer in whose presence the interview is held."

These rules were, with a single exception, strictly enforced. Those of us whose quarters were contiguous, were suffered to pass backwards and forwards, at will, provided we did not step off the pavement, which ran around the enclosure. But we could not visit the quarters of those who were on the opposite side of the Fort, without permission of the Sergeant of the Guard. We were only allowed to walk for one hour in the morning, and one hour in the afternoon, upon the little patch of ground within the Fort. Why the privilege of walking there, at all times, was denied us, it is hard to conjecture. The space inside was so small, that, when we took our afternoon's exercise, it was literally crowded. The walls surrounding it were three stories high, and there was but one point at which egress was possible, and that was just at the guard-house, where the guard was always on duty. It was but a wanton and senseless restriction to confine us to the pavement in front of our quarters. At first, the prisoners had to clean their own rooms, and to perform all other similar menial offices. Afterwards, they were allowed, for an hour or two in the morning, to employ one of the soldiers, who, being unable to speak or understand the English language, may be presumed to have been unfit for military duty, as he certainly was for any other.

The most private communications regarding domestic affairs or business having to be subjected to the criticism of Lieutenant WOOD, we preferred to be silent concerning such matters, be the consequences what they might. Such were the regulations to which the Government, or its agents, thought proper to subject its victims.

Our complaints of the manner in which we were treated, had been persistent and decided; and from time to time, released prisoners made them known to the public through the columns of various newspapers. One of these statements appeared in the New York *Herald*, of October 24th. It did not contain a line that was not strictly true. On the 26th, the following letters were published in the same journal, I presume, by Colonel BURKE's directions.

The first was addressed to the United States' Marshal in New York. It was dated, the *Herald* said, on the 9th of October, 1861.

"SIR:—I have the honor to enclose herewith, a list of articles necessary for the State prisoners confined at this Post, which you will please send me at your earliest convenience.

"The water being almost entirely out, you will please send me a water-boat, with a supply of water to fill two cisterns, which will last until we have rain enough to obviate the difficulty, You cannot comply too soon, as it is an immediate necessity.

"List of articles necessary for the comfort of prisoners:

"100 blankets, 200 sheets, 200 pillow cases, 50 single mattresses, 50 pillows, 50 iron bedsteads, 50 arm chairs, 20 small tables, 50 washstands, 25 washbowls and pitchers, 10 small oval stoves and pipe, 50 wooden buckets, 100 tin cups, 250 yards of rope carpet for laying on brick floors. I take this opportunity to inform you that the ship's galley and other articles furnished by you, are very satisfactory, and answer the purpose for which they were required.

"I am, very respectfully, your obedient servant,

"CHARLES O. WOOD,"

" *Second Lieutenant of Infantry,*

"Commanding Post.

" Approved:—MARTIN BURKE,

Lieutenant-Colonel, Commanding

" *Forts Hamilton and La Fayette.*"

"HEADQUARTERS, FORT HAMILTON, *October 24th*, 1861.

"ROBERT MURRAY, ESQ.,

" *United States Marshal*, New York.

"My attention was drawn to a statement in the *Herald* of this morning, from a prisoner lately released from Fort La Fayette. Now I wish to call your attention to the same article, and submit its further consideration to your judgment.

"You and I both know how hard the Government has striven to make these prisoners comfortable, and if in the whirlpool of business, they have been apparently neglected, we can both testify as to the present ample preparations which are being made, not only to render them comfortable, but even to put it beyond the complaint of some who would be unreasonable.

"In regard to myself, I can simply say, that I have, to the utmost of my ability, tried to do my duty, alike to the Government and the prisoners.

"Lieutenant Wood is unceasing in his care and watchfulness, and as you well know, ready at any time to do all he can for the comfort of those under his charge.

"With regard to improper and false communications from released prisoners, if such there are, it is a question for the Honorable Secretary of State to decide how far such communications invalidate the parole of the person or persons making them.

"Very respectfully, your obedient servant,

"MARTIN BURKE,

"*Lieutenant-Colonel Commanding.*"

It will be observed that Lieutenant Wood's requisition was only made the day after the date of the "remonstrance" which we had sent to Mr. Lincoln. Whether it would have been made at all but for that remonstrance, may well be doubted. We had been over two weeks in Fort La Fayette before Lieutenant Wood thought proper to give any such evidence of that "care and watchfulness" which Colonel Burke attributed to him. "How hard the Government had striven" to make the prisoners comfortable may be judged by the foregoing narrative, and from the fact that the articles for which Lieutenant Wood called on Marshal Murray, only reached the Fort sometime about the date of Colonel Burke's letter, and we had then been imprisoned there nearly a month. That Colonel Burke made any special efforts to do his duty to the prisoners, is utterly untrue. He paid a visit to the Fort about the 5th of August, and did not appear there again until about the 26th of October, and but for facts which I shall subsequently mention, it is not likely that he would have paid the latter visit at all. Had he chosen to inspect our quarters more frequently, or give us opportunities of preferring our complaints, he might, had he so pleased, have mitigated, in very many respects, the rigors of our imprisonment. I may add, that no "communications from released prisoners," that I ever saw, were in any particular, untrue or exaggerated, and the promptitude with which Col. BURKE threw out his sinister suggestion to the Marshal, shows how anxious he was for the suppression of all such information.

Our correspondence was subjected to the strictest scrutiny, and letters written by the prisoners were frequently returned to them, and generally because they contained facts which the Government did not desire should become known, or reflections on the Government itself. On one occasion Lieut. WOOD returned to me a letter which I had written to my wife. No reason was assigned for this; but I was forced to the conclusion that it was sent back because Lieut. WOOD chose to consider it too long. It was a small sheet of note paper. There was nothing in the contents to which he could object, and as two letters of the same length as mine, were returned to the writers that morning, with a message from Lieut. WOOD that they were too long, I inferred that mine was sent back for a similar cause. To such annoyances we were continually subjected. At times our condition became so unendurable, that finding our complaints unheeded, we expressed our sense of the indignities put upon us, in perfectly plain language. On one occasion, when outraged by some fresh act of harshness or impertinence, I wrote a letter to a friend, in which, after describing our situation, I used this language:

"To have imprisoned men solely on account of their political opinions, is enough to bring eternal infamy on every individual connected with the Administration; but the manner in which we have been treated since our confinement, is, if possible, even more disgraceful to them. I should have supposed that, if the Government chose to confine citizens because their sentiments were distasteful to it, it would have contented itself with keeping them in custody, but would have put them in tolerably comfortable quarters * * * * * * * * If I had been told twelve months ago, that the American people would ever have permitted their rulers, under any pretence whatever, to establish such a despotism as I have lived to witness. I should have indignantly denied the assertion; and if I had been then told, that officers of the Army would ever consent to be the instruments to carry out the behests of a vulgar dictator, I should have predicted that they would rather have stripped their epaulets from their shoulders. But we live to learn; and I have learned much in the past few months."

This letter was returned to me the next morning, and on the following day one of the sergeants handed me a letter addressed by Colonel BURKE, to Lieutenant WOOD, which he said the latter had ordered him to read to me particularly, and to the other prisoners. I was unable to procure a copy of this letter, but remember the tenor of it. Colonel BURKE expressed his surprise that I should have attempted to make him and Lieutenant WOOD the medium through which to cast reflections on their superior officers. He was also pleased to say that as my family had always borne a gentlemanly character in Maryland he had not expected that I would be guilty of conduct "so indelicate, to use no stronger terms." He concluded by insisting that the Government had been, and would be unremitting in its exertions to make us comfortable.

I immediately sent him this note:

"FORT LA FAYETTE, *October* 23*d*.

"LIEUTENANT-COLONEL BURKE,

"SIR:

"Lieutenant WOOD, has communicated to me the contents of your note to him of this date. Permit me to say, in reply to your allusions to the course I have thought proper to pursue, that you mistake me much if you suppose (as you seem to do) that a mere desire to embarrass or annoy you, or the officers under you, has prompted me to write the letters which have been returned to me. The fact that little or nothing has been done to make me or my fellow prisoners decently comfortable, is self-evident to any one who chooses to inspect our quarters, and it was on that account that I chose to speak in terms of indignant denunciation of those who are responsible for the privations I suffer. If I made, or sought to make, the officers of the garrison the 'instruments' to convey my complaints, it was because I am denied any other alternative. The invidious allusions which you have deemed it necessary to make in regard to me, I need not, and do not propose, now, to discuss. But you will permit me to remind you that if you have duties to discharge, I have rights to vindicate. The only one of these which has not been absolutely destroyed, is the right of free speech within the narrow bounds of my prison, and this it is my duty and purpose to defend to the last. In the exercise of this poor privilege I wrote the letters which I knew were to pass into your hands. As you have forwarded to the Adjutant-General the correspondence between Lieutenant Wood and yourself, I beg that you will do me the justice to forward also this note. I remain,

"Your obedient servant,

"F. K. HOWARD."

To the foregoing note, he wrote this reply:

"HEADQUARTERS, FORT HAMILTON,

"New York Harbor, 24th October, 1861.

"SIR:

"Please say to Mr. HOWARD, that I cheerfully forward his note of the 23d inst. to Colonel TOWNSEND, agreeably to his request.

"However much the efforts of this Government have fallen short of the expectations of the prisoners, to make them as comfortable as they may desire, still I must say that every exertion is being made by the Government for that purpose, and such exertions will certainly be continued.

"Very respectfully, your obedient servant,

"MARTIN BURKE,

"Colonel-Commanding."

"LIEUTENANT WOOD,

"Commanding Fort La Fayette."

My father, to whom Colonel BURKE's letter had been read, wrote to the Secretary of War, denying Colonel BURKE's allegations, and charging him with neglect of duty.

6

"Fort La Fayette, *October 23d*, 1861.

"Hon. SIMON CAMERON, *Sec'y of War*,

"Washington, D. C.

"Sir:

"The Orderly-Sergeant has this morning, by order of the Commanding Officer of this Post, read to me in presence of a number of persons, a letter from Colonel Martin Burke to Lieutenant C. O. Wood, written in reply to a communication from the Lieutenant to him. Copies of both of these letters, Colonel Burke states he has forwarded to Washington. I have asked for a copy of the Colonel's letter, but have not learned whether it will be given. In that letter, which is evidently intended as a rebuke to some of those confined here, Colonel Burke has undertaken to allude to the character and standing which my family have borne, for the purpose of introducing an offensive imputation, that one member of it has acted in a manner unbecoming a gentleman. This charge, I claim the right distinctly and directly to repudiate, and I have also to demand that an inquiry be made under your authority into the conduct of Colonel Burke and Lieutenant Wood, in relation to their treatment of those confined at this place. I now formally charge Colonel Burke with conduct unbecoming an officer, and also with neglect of duty. He has not, so far as any prisoner here is aware, been within this Fort since on or about the 5th day of August last, and in undertaking to judge of Lieutenant Wood's manner of discharging his duty towards the prisoners under his charge, he must have acted upon the statements of that officer himself. The Surgeon of the post and one other officer from Fort Hamilton, have occasionally exchanged a few words with some of the prisoners, but whenever any of the latter have attempted to make any representations to them of our condition and treatment, both of those officers have declared that those matters are not in any manner, within the sphere of their duties. There has therefore, been no inspection of this prison, in which upwards of one hundred prisoners are confined, which would enable Colonel Burke to judge of the accuracy of the reports which he may have received. In the absence of all such means of knowledge or information, Colonel Burke has stated in an official letter, that Lieutenant Wood, an officer under his command, has 'devoted his whole time to promoting the comfort of prisoners' here, or words to that effect. This statement, I charge to be not warranted by the facts, and to be entirely incorrect. I charge and

aver, that Lieutenant WOOD has not only not devoted all, or even
much of his time, to the promoting of our comfort, but that on the
contrary, he has neither in his general bearing, nor in his conduct
towards those consigned to his custody, paid that attention to their
comfort, which even under the circumstances which the Government
deemed sufficient to warrant their imprisonment, they have a right
to demand. The immediate cause of the rebuke attempted to be
administered to us by Colonel BURKE, was a letter written to a
friend by Mr. F. K. HOWARD, my son. However strong may have
been the language used in that letter, it was the natural expression
of feelings which are shared by every prisoner here, whose opinion
I have heard. Among these are many gentlemen of as high
character and standing as any in the country. No intimation has
been given by Colonel BURKE, that any specific fact stated in the
letter was not true. Should he controvert a single one, my
relations to the writer of the letter, and the mention made by
Colonel BURKE in his official communication, of my family, to say
nothing of the assurances voluntarily tendered to me by you in
Fort McHenry, as to the mode in which the Government considered me as entitled to be treated, justify me in demanding an
opportunity to substantiate it. Having already addressed to you
three communications, from this place, of which no notice appears
to have been taken, I should not again have troubled you, but
that the issue I have now to make with Colonel BURKE, involves matters of a personal character to myself, and that I make direct
charges against him and Lieutenant WOOD, derogatory to their official
positions, as officers of the army.

"I hope, therefore, I may not be mistaken, in trusting that
this communication may receive your early and serious attention.

"I am sir, your obedient servant,

"CHARLES HOWARD."

As usual, this letter was unnoticed by the authorities in
Washington.

In the miserable place which I have attempted to describe, we passed the period between September 26th and
October 30th. The batteries were very dark when the doors
were closed, and very cold when the doors were open. We
were locked up every night from dusk until sunrise; and
lights had to be put out at 9½ o'clock. In such a crowded

place it was almost impossible to read or write. We found it difficult sometimes to keep ourselves warm enough even with the aid of overcoats. At times again, the atmosphere of the room would be positively stifling. Some one or more of the inmates were constantly under medical treatment, and it may be imagined how noisome and unhealthy the room often was. As prisoners were, from time to time, discharged from the casemates, the remaining inmates would invite one or more of those in the gun batteries to fill the vacancies, permission to do so being first asked of the Sergeant of the Guard. These invitations were given, not because the casemates were less crowded than the batteries, but because the first stranger who should be brought in, would certainly be put in the place of the prisoner who had been last discharged, and, as the casemates were to be kept filled to their utmost capacity, those occupying them preferred to have their friends and acquaintances for their companions. Small and crowded as the casemates were, they were, nevertheless, a little more comfortable than the batteries, from having fire-places and wooden floors. I was fortunate enough to get into one of these casemates after I had been some two weeks in the Fort.

About ten days before we left Fort La Fayette, Lieutenant Wood chose to make the prisoners responsible for the drunkenness of one of the soldiers, and prohibited the further use of liquor, of any kind, among the prisoners. It was discovered a few days afterwards, that some of the soldiers had stolen some of our liquor from the room in which Lieutenant Wood kept it, and to which the prisoners had no access. It was also discovered that the soldiers got liquor from the Long Island side, one of the crew of the boat having been detected in smuggling it into the Fort for their use. These facts sufficiently accounted for the drunkenness of the soldiers, but Lieutenant Wood did not, on that account, relax his new rule. While we were allowed the use of liquor, no abuse of the privilege came under my observation, nor do I believe there was any. Just before the new restriction was imposed on us, I had received from New York two small boxes of liquor containing a dozen-and-a-half bottles, which passed, as usual, into Lieutenant Wood's keeping. The prohibition which followed, prevented my using any of it, and, when we were about leaving, I requested Lieutenant Wood, through one of the Sergeants, to send it on with me in charge of the officer who would have us in custody. This he did not do, and I never saw more of it. One or two of the prisoners afterwards received, at Fort Warren, the liquors that they left at Fort La Fayette, and one of the officers at the former Post informed me that there were some boxes on the bill of lading which did not reach Fort Warren. Whether any of my stores were among these boxes, I am unable to say. I only know that I never received the liquor which Lieutenant Wood had, and that many of my companions suffered in the same way.

Those of our friends who obtained passes to visit the Fort, did so with great difficulty. The government seemed to have a strong disposition to exclude all strangers from the place. Six weeks before my arrest, I had made every effort to procure a permit to see my father, but could not succeed in getting one. Some New York politicians, however, were more favored. One of them, especially, Mr. WILLIAM H. LUDLOW, could enter the Fort at his pleasure, and see whom he pleased. On several occasions when he made his visits, he sent for different individuals, to whom he represented himself as possessing great influence at Washington, and offered to try and procure their release, provided he was paid for it. What he received altogether I do not know ; but I do know that he received two retaining fees, namely—$100 from one gentleman, and $150 from another. From the latter he had a promise of a contingent fee of $1,000. I do not believe he rendered any service to his clients, both of whom were taken to Fort Warren and exchanged or released nearly four months afterwards.

The private soldiers at Fort La Fayette were worthy followers of their commanding officer. They were uniformly as brutal in their manners towards the prisoners as they dared to be. The Sergeants, however, who were there when I was, were generally civil, and were as kind

as they had an opportunity of being. But, if the situation
of those who were fortunate enough to enjoy good health
was almost insupportable, the condition of the sick was
far worse. No provision whatever was made for them.
Men suffering from various diseases were compelled to
remain in their close and damp quarters, and struggle
through as best they could. One man, "a political prisoner," had an acute attack of pneumonia, and lay for
ten days in a damp, dark gun battery, with some thirty
other prisoners. One of the privateersmen was dangerously
ill with the same disease in the casemate in which so
many of them were huddled together. When I obtained
permission to carry him some little luxuries, I found him
lying on the floor upon two blankets in a high fever,
and without even a pillow under his head. He would have
remained in the same condition had not the "political
prisoners" relieved his necessities. It was not until he
seemed to be drawing rapidly towards his end, that he was
sent to a Hospital, somewhere on Staten Island.

Another man, a "political prisoner," manifested symp-
toms of insanity. His friends, and some of the physicians,
who were among the prisoners, called Lieutenant WOOD's
attention to the case. He treated the statement with
contemptuous indifference at the time, but a few days
afterwards we learned that the man had been sent to the
guard-house. Here he became thoroughly insane. Instead of being sent instantly to an Asylum, he was kept,
for some ten days, in the guard-house, and in double
irons. His friends were not allowed free access to him,
and surrounded by strange soldiers, he was, at times,
apparently in an agony of dread. His shrieks were
fearful, and one night, as he imagined he was about to
be murdered, his screams were painfully startling to hear.
In some of these paroxysms, he was actually gagged by the
soldiers. He was subsequently removed to an Asylum,
where, I believe, he eventually improved or recovered. A
letter, written by one of our number to the counsel of the
unfortunate man, in Baltimore, urging the exercise of his
influence with the Government, on behalf of the sufferer,

was not allowed to reach its destination, although directed to the care of Lieut. General SCOTT.

Among the pettier annoyances we underwent, the trouble we had about our washing may be mentioned. At first, we were allowed to send our clothes over to Long Island, where they were well enough washed, but for some reason best known to himself, Lieutenant WOOD interfered, and determined to have the washing done inside of the Fort, under his own supervision. It must have been a very fair speculation for him, for his charges were high, and the work was so carelessly performed, that he must have employed the fewest hands possible to do it. What he charged me by the piece, I cannot say, for he helped himself to his bill before he handed over my money to the officer who escorted us to Fort Warren. Probably it would not have been altogether safe to have demanded an account, for one of the Sergeants was put under arrest for complaining, as he stated to the prisoners, of Lieutenant WOOD'S prices for washing. On one occasion, Lieutenant WOOD, in full view of the prisoners, kicked one of his boat's crew from the door of his own quarters, and continued the assault until the man had retreated almost the whole length of the balcony upon that side of the Fort. I mention this as an illustration of his mode of dealing with his subordinates. Of the propriety and manliness of such a proceeding, on the part of the Commanding Officer, others can judge for themselves.

Many of the prisoners had friends and acquaintances in New York, but most of these were either afraid, or did not care to show any kindness or attention to parties who were under the ban of a suspicious and tyrannical Government. Some few people in that city, had the courage and inclination to render us any service in their power, and prominent among these was Mr. CRANSTON, of the New York Hotel; but the number of those who thus acted was singularly small.

I cannot take leave of this portion of my narrative without recording the obligations under which the prisoners in Fort La Fayette must ever remain, to Mrs. GEO. S. GELSTON and Mr. FRANCIS HOPKINS, who lived on Long Island just oppo-

site the Fort. They were unwearied in their efforts to alleviate our situation. Day after day, for weeks and months
together, they manifested their good will in the most generous and substantial way. Food for those who were too poor to
buy a decent meal, delicacies of all kinds for the sick, luxuries
for others—all these were supplied by Mrs. GELSTON, with a
bountiful and untiring hand. To her tender sympathy and
generosity, very many of the prisoners were indebted for
comforts which were absolutely necessary to enable them to
endure the privations to which they were exposed, and I
know I but inadequately fulfil the wishes of every one of
the former inmates of Fort La Fayette, in thus giving public
expression to thanks which they had no opportunity to
return to their good friends in person.

It is scarcely necessary to say, that our opinions as to the
sort of resistance we should offer to our oppressors, underwent no change in consequence of our cruel imprisonment
in Fort La Fayette. I found on reaching there, that my
father and most of his companions had taken the same view
of their duty under the circumstances, as we had done ; and
with every day's prolongation of our sufferings, we were
the more and more convinced, that with a despotism so
atrocious, we ought to make no compromise.

The Steamboat "State of Maine."

On the afternoon of the 28th of October, we were notified to prepare to leave Fort La Fayette on the following morning. We were then locked up in the various casemates and batteries for the rest of that day. The next morning our baggage was sent out to the wharf, we being still kept in close confinement, and a little after mid-day our baggage was brought back, and we were informed that the boat would not be ready that day. We were kept under lock and key all that day, and only permitted to go out to dinner. There was no conceivable reason for this last act of insolent harshness. On the morning of the 30th, we left the Fort on a small steamer, with a file of soldiers, and were carried up to Fort Columbus, on Governor's Island, and alongside of the steamer "State of Maine," which was lying at the wharf. She was a very ordinary looking river steamer, very low in the water, and very dirty. Her upper forward deck was covered with soldiers. She had been engaged in transporting soldiers and horses, and an experienced sea captain of our party, who managed to evade the sentinels and go over the vessel, informed me that between decks forward of the shaft, she was perfectly filthy. There were about one hundred and ten of us, and we were sent on board of the "State of Maine," and directed to pass into the upper after cabin. This cabin was long and dark, and in it there were about twenty-two or three small state rooms, each containing two berths. It opened, aft, upon a covered deck, which

7

was so small that, when our party collected there, it was considerably over-crowded. Just beneath the deck on which we were was the dining saloon, along the sides of which ran a double tier of berths. There may have been about twenty or twenty-five of these altogether. The whole after part of the vessel could not decently accommodate the one hundred and ten prisoners then on board. To our astonishment we learned that not only were we to take on board some seventeen "political prisoners" from Fort Columbus, but that the officers and soldiers who had been taken prisoners at Fort Hatteras were to join us also. These numbered six hundred and forty-five. Remonstrance or complaint was useless. These additional prisoners were marched on board, the officers and "political prisoners" being sent to the after part of the boat with us, and the privates being packed in forward of the cabin, wherever it was possible for them to find standing room.

We did not get away from Fort Columbus until about 4½, P.M. While we were still lying at the wharf, it seems to have occurred to some of those in charge of us, that it was part of their duty to offer us something to eat. A large wicker basket, lined with tin, was then brought up full of water. It had been made to hold dirty plates and dishes, and had been used for that purpose, apparently, time out of mind, on the steamer. A soldier then brought up a box of crackers, and another appeared with a tin plate, which was several times replenished, containing large square pieces of boiled pork. Nine out of ten of these pieces were solid lumps of pure fat. A couple of old dirty-looking horse buckets of coffee were also provided. Such was the dinner furnished us. After this I saw no more of the pork, nor do I think there was any more on board, at least for the prisoners. Hunger compelled some of the prisoners to try and swallow the masses of blubber which were offered them, but many were unequal to the effort. A large proportion of the party dined, therefore, on crackers and water. When we started we had on board one hundred and twenty-seven "political prisoners," six hundred and forty-five prisoners of war, and one hundred Federal soldiers, besides the officers and crew of the steamer. I subsequently learned that the only stores put on board for our subsistence consisted of one thousand and six pounds of hard bread, one hundred and twenty-eight pounds of coffee, and two hundred and fifty-eight pounds of sugar.

Thus loaded down almost to the water's edge, we headed for Long Island Sound. The discomfort of our situation cannot be described. Moreover, we all knew, for the naval officers among us had so said, and the officers of the boat admitted, that the vessel was, in her then condition, utterly unseaworthy, and that, if a moderate gale should catch us at sea, the chances were largely in favor of our going to the bottom.

About dusk I heard that supper had been prepared in the dining saloon, for the officers who had us in charge, and that, as far as it would go, those of us who chose to pay for it, could partake of it. It was at the same time stated, that the officers of the boat had received no notice of the number of the prisoners she was to carry, and had not made the slightest provision for them. Under such circumstances, but very few of us could get a single meal in the dining saloon. By dint of great patience and perseverance, I succeeded in getting some supper about nine o'clock at night. The next day, after many ineffectual efforts, I managed to get a very late breakfast, and that was the last meal I got from the officers of the boat or Government. I was far better off, however, than the mass of my companions; for Mrs. GELSTON again stood our friend. She had heard we were to leave Fort La Fayette, and had thoughtfully sent to those occupying the casemate in which I was, a huge basket of provisions for our journey. It contained pheasants, chickens, tongues, pies and other delicacies, and one of my room-mates, Mr. WARFIELD, and myself, consented, or perhaps volunteered, to take it under our especial charge during the journey. On these stores, I and my former room-mates lived for the ensuing two days, sharing them, however, as far as we could, with other friends. But our supplies were wholly insufficient to meet any but the most limited demand, and we could extend our invitations to but few. Most of the prisoners had to put up with the hard bread and coffee, during the two days and nights we remained on board.

Just before dark, the clerk of the boat came on the after-deck to distribute the keys of the few state-rooms assigned to us, which until then had been kept locked. The North Carolina officers had the berths in the dining saloon. There were, as already mentioned, about twenty-two state-rooms altogether, in the upper after cabin, and one or two of these were used for different purposes by the officers of the boat, and one or two others could accommodate but one person each. It was obvious that not more than one-third of us would get any beds. Here again I was very fortunate, for I happened to be standing by Governor MOREHEAD, to whom the clerk gave the first key, and I was able to secure one. Those who failed to obtain berths, either in the dining saloon or state-rooms, and they constituted a very large majority of the party, had no alternative, but to drop down wherever they could, and try to sleep. After those who had beds had retired, the cabin presented a scene that no man who was present will be likely to forget. It was densely packed with men, in every possible position. Upon each of the hard wooden settees two or three persons had contrived to stow themselves in half recumbent positions, that were little likely to afford them the desired rest. Those who had chairs were sleeping on them, some sitting bolt upright, and some leaning back against the sides of the cabin. But many could get neither chairs nor places on the settees, and these were lying or sitting upon the floor. Over the latter had been strewn bread and pieces of fat pork, all of which being saturated with the expectorations of numberless tobacco chewers, had been trampled into a consistent mass of filth, by the feet of one hundred and fifty men. Some of the unfortunates, whom absolute weariness had compelled to lie down on the floor, were lucky enough, as they esteemed themselves, to obtain some newspapers, which they spread between the dirt and their persons; others had to take the floor as they found it, and the vacant spaces were so limited that many were not even allowed a choice of places. As for the prisoners of war, the privates, they seem to have slept, if they slept at all, wherever they could manage to stretch themselves. We were not suffered to go among them, but I could see from the door of the dining saloon, the morning after we started, that they were lying about between decks, on piles of coal, coils of rope, or the bare floor.

We reached Fort Warren about dusk on the evening of the 31st, and Colonel JUSTIN DIMICK, who commanded the Post, came on board. · He said that he had only expected one hundred and ten prisoners, that not the slightest notice of the coming of the prisoners of war, had been given, and that he was wholly unprepared to receive us. He, however, ordered some three hundred of the North Carolina soldiers ashore, and said the rest of us must remain that night on board. Thus we had another cheerless and wretched night to look forward to. It passed like the previous one, and we were only too glad when day dawned, well knowing that whatever might happen, our situation could not be made worse.

That morning before we left the boat, I vainly endeavored to procure a glass of drinkable water. There was none to be had on board. The only supply of water left, was stale and foul and was used for washing, though not fit for that purpose. I was too thirsty to be particular, and having disguised the color and flavor of a glassful by pouring into it a teaspoonful of essence of ginger, I made shift to swallow it. I then breakfasted on the scraps which remained in our basket, and prepared to go ashore.

This account of the privations to which we were subjected on that occasion, I have neither over-stated nor over-colored. On a convict ship our position could have been no worse, and even on such a vessel, more regard would be manifested for the safety of the prisoners than was shown for ours. And all this was endured by numbers of gentlemen who would be disparaged by being compared, in point of character, intelligence and position, with Mr. LINCOLN, Mr. STANTON, or Mr. SEWARD. It was an extremely fortunate thing, that the weather was fine, and the sea calm, after we passed out of the Sound. Wretched as our situation was, it would have been aggravated ten-fold, had many of the prisoners suffered from sea sickness. We were, however, spared such addition to our troubles. I need not therefore surmise, how miserable in such a case, our lot would have been, nor what would have been the inevitable result of our being overtaken by such a gale as set in the very night after we reached Fort Warren. With a very little forethought and trouble, and a very slight expenditure of money on the part of the Government, or of those of its officers who were charged with our transportation to Fort Warren, our journey might have been made in tolerable decency, if not comfort. As it was, we were treated with as little consideration as cattle. The brutality that characterised the higher officers of the Government, seemed, as far as we could then judge, to be equally conspicuous in most of their subordinates.

Fort Warren.

WHEN we reached Fort Warren, late in the afternoon of the 31st, Colonel DIMICK came on board, as I have stated, and informed us that he had only expected about a hundred "political prisoners." He invited several gentlemen to go ashore and see the quarters he had set apart for us. Among these were Commodore BARRON, Mayor BROWN,. and Messrs. FAULKNER, CHARLES HOWARD and KANE. They hurriedly inspected the various rooms by candle-light, and after about an hour's absence they returned. That night they selected their quarters and their room-mates, as Colonel DIMICK had requested them to do.

About 10 o'clock the following morning we landed, and were marched into the Fort, where the roll was called, and we were shown to our respective quarters. The Fort is situated on an island containing forty-three acres, nearly the whole of which is covered by the fortifications. The interior work is built in the most substantial manner, of granite, and encloses a space of some five or six acres. It is an irregular structure, which it is impossible for me to describe accurately. The five principal sides are each about three hundred feet long. Two of these sides are divided into deep casemates, on a level with, and opening on the parade-ground. One other side contains rooms intended for officers' quarters. There were ten of these rooms on a level with, and looking out on the parade-ground, and immediately in the rear of these were ten more fronting on the space between the curtain and an exterior work. Beneath these twenty rooms, both in front and rear, there were twenty more of the same size as those above, the inner or front ones being, of course, basement rooms, and opening upon an area about seven feet wide and ten or twelve deep, and those in the rear looking out on the space between the interior and exterior works above mentioned, which was below the level of the inside enclosure. Between the front and rear rooms, above and below, there were also two very small dark rooms, intended, I presume, for store-rooms. All the interior or front rooms were lighted by large windows, and those in the rear by narrow loop holes, about six inches wide, at the outer edge, and four or five feet high. The upper rooms were all neatly finished, and those in front were very light and airy. The lower rooms had cement floors, and were much less desirable. Sixteen of the rooms I have attempted to describe, were assigned to the "political prisoners," and the officers who were prisoners of war, viz.: four front rooms opening on the parade-ground, and four immediately beneath them, and eight just in the rear of these, together with the smaller rooms or closets which separated the front and rear rooms. One large, long casemate, in another side of the Fort, was devoted to the same purpose. Commodore BARRON and several of the army officers with him, and Marshal KANE, selected one of the four upper front rooms; the North Carolina officers of the highest rank another; the Baltimore Police Commissioners another; and the Mayor of Baltimore and Messrs. MOREHEAD and FAULKNER the fourth. These several parties having, in accordance with Colonel DIMICK's request, made choice of their rooms, also selected as their companions, in their new quarters, those who had been their room-mates at Fort Columbus and Fort La Fayette. I thus found myself again among my old room-mates. The other prisoners, generally choosing their own room-mates, were quartered in the other rooms and in the casemate before mentioned. The crowded condition of the room I occupied will illustrate the situation of our fellow prisoners. This room was nineteen-and-a-half by fifteen feet, and one of the little closets of which we had the use, was ten by ten-and-a-half feet. Into this room and closet, nine of us were crowded. So close together were our beds, that it would have been impossible to have put another one in the room without blocking up the doors. There was scarcely space enough for another, even in the middle of the floor. Those who got into the long casemate were far worse off than their other fellow prisoners. This casemate was, I should suppose, less than fifty feet long and less than twenty wide, and so crowded was it, that the inmates were compelled to sleep in bunks which were arranged one above the other, in three tiers. They had also to cook their meals in the same room.

When we were installed in our quarters we began to look around to see what sort of provision had been made for us. As we had been told that at least a hundred of us had been expected, we naturally took it for granted that something had been done to make us tolerably comfortable. Our former experience ought to have prevented us from entertaining any such hopes, but we were not long under any delusion. No preparation had apparently been made for one single prisoner, except that fires were kindled in the various rooms. Colonel DIMICK, whose demeanor towards us was on all occasions that of a gentleman, seemed to be annoyed at the position in which he found himself. He informed us of his inability to provide for us decently, and expressed his regret at the fact. But his good feeling could not much alleviate our situation. Not a bedstead, bed, blanket or chair was then furnished any of us. Those of us who had carried on the bedding we had purchased at Fort La Fayette, were able to lend a few articles to our friends, but the great majority of the prisoners were forced to sleep upon the floor, upon their great coats and the few cloaks and shawls they happened to have or could borrow. This state of things continued two or three weeks, at the end of which time, Colonel DIMICK managed to have the furniture, which had been so tardily provided for us at Fort La Fayette, sent on to Fort Warren. In the mean time, many had, at their own expense, supplied themselves from Boston with necessary articles,

8

but the others had to shift for themselves as they best could, until the arrival of the furniture from our former prison. The day we landed, the only dinner provided for us consisted of a barrel of crackers and a couple of raw hams, which were placed on the head of a flour barrel, in front of our quarters. We were informed that the Government would allow us the ordinary soldiers' rations, but that we would have to cook them ourselves, and a place would be given us for the purpose. Mr. HALL, the purveyor for the laborers and officers at the Post, agreed to furnish us that evening with supper. It consisted of cold, boiled salt beef, bread and bad coffee, which however, we were hungry enough to eat with considerable relish. This was the only meal we had that day, or until noon the day following. Not knowing exactly how we could manage our rations after they should be distributed to us, a number of us by Colonel DIMICK's permission, requested Mr. HALL to furnish us two meals a day, at least until we could make some other arrangement. This he agreed to do at the rate of one dollar a day each, and a good business he must have made of it, for scantier and worse entertainment we had never seen provided at anything like half the price. We were forced, however, to continue this arrangement for a week, at the end of which time we took matters into our own hands. We obtained the use of two casemates and cooking stoves, and established two clubs or messes, and engaged some of the North Carolina prisoners to cook and wait in the mess-room, and also to attend to our quarters. As there was a Government boat running regularly between the Fort and Boston, we ordered daily supplies of meats, milk, and vegetables, and with the addition of our rations, were enabled to live with reasonable comfort. After the North Carolina prisoners were exchanged, we from time to time, got servants from Boston, almost invariably foreigners, and continued, though at an increased expense, to live as we had previously done.

In speaking of our treatment, I speak solely of the "political" or "State prisoners." As I know nothing of the way in which prisoners of war are entitled to be, or usually are, dealt with, I have nothing to say upon that point. I will merely state, that the North Carolina prisoners, numbering about six hundred, exclusive of their commissioned officers, were confined in eight casemates. They were thus terribly crowded. During the first two or three days they had scarcely anything to eat. I do not know the cause of this, but the fact is, that they absolutely suffered from hunger. Afterwards they received their rations regularly, and large boilers were placed in front of their quarters for them to cook in. These were in the open air, and not in any way sheltered, and the men had to cook there in all kinds of weather, during the time they remained, which was until they were exchanged in February, 1862.

In front of the range of rooms occupied by the "political prisoners," and about ten yards off, sentinels were placed, and beyond them we were not allowed to go. The officers who were prisoners of war, were permitted to walk about the whole island, both within and without the Fort, on their parole; but we were confined to the space some hundred yards long, by ten wide, between our quarters and the line of sentinels just mentioned. This regulation was enforced for nearly six months, and as we understood at the time, was specifically directed by the Government. During that time, we were kept strictly within those narrow bounds. Why men who were taken with arms in their hands were less rigorously treated than we, was obvious. The Confederate Government could exact certain rights for them, but there was no power or law in this part of the country, to protect us. The day after our arrival, I wrote to my wife this hurried account of our journey from Fort La Fayette.

"Fort Warren, Boston Harbor, *Saturday, Nov. 2d.*

"We have arrived here safely, and a more uncomfortable set of human beings have never, I trust, been collected before in these quarters. We left Fort La Fayette on Wednesday morning, and together with the prisoners from Fort Columbus, came here on one of the Sound steamers. There were about four times as many on board as the vessel could accommodate, and the only food which the Gov-

ernment provided was bread and fat pork and a liquid called coffee.—
I saw the most prominent gentlemen of Maryland, Kentucky and
Virginia drinking what purported to be coffee, out of a dirty horse-
bucket, while water was served out to them from a large tin, such as
is used to hold the greasy plates after dinner. Pieces of fat about
two inches square, were handed round to those who could swallow
them, and a man's fingers constituted the table furniture. A number
of elderly gentlemen could not at night find a place to sit; and scores
of my friends slept for two nights upon the floors, which were the
filthiest that you are ever likely to see. At this place no provision
whatever had been made for us. Many of the rooms are not fit for
the accommodation of human beings in the winter months in this
climate. No beds have been furnished, and none are to be—a sack
of straw being the only thing which the Government will supply.
Even such bedding as this has not arrived. We have been here
twenty-four hours, and most of the party have lived on a little raw
ham and bread, and have slept on the floor. Not even a blanket has
been given us. I have managed to get along better than most of my
fellow prisoners, for I brought my mattress and a basket of provisions.
I also was lucky enough to secure a state room. The privations I
have suffered, serious as they were, have been light compared to those
which numbers of my companions have endured. It is now 10
o'clock, and we are as yet vainly trying to get some breakfast, which
a caterer from Boston has agreed to furnish. I thus give you the
brief outlines of this phase of our story. It is not necessary
that I should supply the comments. I will write again when I
have had a little time to look about me. The officers, as far as I can
judge, are polite and kind, which in my late experiences is a novelty.
It has been our misfortune to meet but few, if any, gentlemen, thus
far, and a change in that particular will be grateful."

I give this letter at length, because it was returned to
me by order of Colonel DIMICK, who sent me word that
his instructions prohibited the transmission of any such
intelligence as I had attempted to send my family. It
is evident from the suppression of so simple a statement of
facts, that the Government had determined to resort to
all the means in its power, to prevent the victims of its
tyranny from making their situation known to the public.
We were specifically ordered not to discuss public affairs
in our letters. It is needless to recapitulate all the ad-
monitions we received upon this point. The following

examples will suffice. On the 8th of April, 1862, a letter
was returned to a "political prisoner" with this note, in
Colonel DIMICK's handwriting:

"The Government require the gentlemen at Fort Warren to avoid,
in their correspondence, discussing the differences between the North
and South, or giving any account of the battles between the contend-
ing forces. This letter is, therefore, respectfully returned."

An order relating to the letters of prisoners was posted
in our quarters, on the 10th of April, which concluded
thus:

"Military and political subjects must be avoided in all correspondence.
                           "LIEUT. JAMES S. CASEY, U. S. A.
                                        "Officer in Charge."

Notwithstanding these regulations, we continued to discuss, from time to time, the forbidden subjects, and, as a large
number of letters were to be inspected every day, many,
which were in violation of the above orders, found their
way to our friends. But this happened, I suppose, because
the examining officer had not time to read the letters very
carefully, for the rules were never directly relaxed or
modified.

After we had been a few weeks in Fort Warren, an
order touching the employment of counsel by prisoners,
and signed by Mr. WILLIAM H. SEWARD, the Secretary of
State, was read to us by the United States Marshal for the
District. We were unable to procure an exact copy of
that order, but we afterwards obtained a copy of a similar
one which was read, somewhere about the same time,
to the prisoners then in Fort La Fayette. This latter
order was signed by a Mr. SETH C. HAWLEY, chief clerk
of the Metropolitan Police Commissioners of New York,
who subsequently visited us also. He was acting, as he
stated, under Mr. SEWARD's directions. The order ran as
follows, and was read at Fort La Fayette on 3d Dec., 1861:

" I am instructed by the Secretary of State to inform you that the Department of State of the United States will not recognize any one as an attorney for political prisoners, and will look with distrust upon all applications for release through such channels; and that such applications will be regarded as additional reasons for declining to release the prisoners.

" And further, that if such prisoners wish to make any communication to the Government, they are at liberty, and are requested to make it directly to the State Department.

"SETH C. HAWLEY."

The purport and phraseology of the order read to us in Fort Warren on the 28th of November, and of the above were identical, except that stronger language was used in the former. Instead of being told that the employment of counsel on our behalf, would be regarded as an additional reason " for declining to release " us, we were distinctly notified that any attempt to communicate with the Government through such channels, would be considered a sufficient reason for prolonging our confinement. We were thus precluded from endeavoring to set our respective cases in their proper light before the State Department, even if we had desired, as some of the prisoners did, to pursue that course. We could look for no relief except such as should be voluntarily vouchsafed to us, by what our oppressors were wont to call " the freest and most beneficent government on earth." The privilege of sending our communications " directly to the State Department," was one to which our past experience forbade us to attach much importance. The fate of the communications we had already addressed to the various Government officers, gave us little encouragement to seek redress in that way, and the sequel will show that our view of the matter was correct. The day after the foregoing order had been promulgated, Colonel DIMICK caused this further order to be read to us :

"DEPARTMENT OF STATE, *Washington, Nov.* 27th, 1861.

"COLONEL:

"The Secretary of State has been informed that Mr. WM. H. LUDLOW, has represented to some of the prisoners confined in Fort La Fayette, that he possesses or can use some influence in their behalf, and has made it a ground for obtaining from them money in hand, or engagements for money or other valuable consideration. Discountenancing and repudiating all such practices, the Secretary of State desires that all the State prisoners may understand, that they are expected to revoke all such engagements now existing, and avoid any hereafter, as they can only lend new complications and embarrassments to the cases of prisoners on whose behalf the Government might be disposed to act with liberality. All persons can communicate directly by letter with the Secretary of State through Colonel DIMICK himself, or any unpaid and disinterested agent whom they may find for that purpose.

[Signed]   "WM. H. SEWARD."

What the cause or precise object of this order was, it was difficult to comprehend. Mr. LUDLOW had had the freest access to the prisoners in Fort La Fayette, and he could only have obtained that privilege from Mr. SEWARD himself, whose Department then had us in charge. Why, then, was he so suddenly and publicly denounced? This question we could not and did not much care to solve; but a fact that transpired immediately afterwards, satisfied us that the apparent quarrel between the two was not irreconcileable. At all events, Mr. SEWARD's hostility did not much damage Mr. LUDLOW, for but a week or two had passed, when it was announced that the latter gentleman, whose proceedings had been "discountenanced and repudiated," had received a commission in the Army. He was made a Major, and appointed a member of General DIX's staff, at Baltimore, where he remained until General DIX was assigned another Post. That Mr. SEWARD was animated by a desire to protect us against imposition, or by any other creditable motive, none of us for an instant believed. But whatever may have been his object in excluding Mr. LUDLOW from what might have been supposed to be a profitable field of professional labor, he certainly did not prevent other lawyers from acting on behalf of the prisoners. How many of these employed counsel, or declined to "revoke" pre-existing engagements, I cannot say. But, in two cases, at least, the paid counsel of "political prisoners" in Fort Warren, were in communication with Mr. SEWARD, about and subseqnent to the date of these orders. Mr. REVERDY JOHNSON, was acting for, at least two gentlemen in Fort Warren, whose release he afterwards obtained; and Mr. EVARTS, of New York, was acting, and continued long after to act, as counsel for another, and was, as such, in communication with the Government.

From time to time, offers were made to different prisoners to discharge them conditionally. Sometimes an oath of allegiance, which bound the party taking it to support the "United States Government," notwithstanding any action which his State might take, was proposed as the price of his release. This was almost uniformly declined. Then various forms of parole were proposed, which bound the respective parties either not to go into the Seceded States, or not to go into the Border States, or not to correspond with any one in any of those States, or not to take up arms against the Government. The simplest parole, in form, merely imposed an obligation not to give "aid and comfort to the enemies in hostility against the United States;". but, as any discussion of the corruption or imbecility of the Administration was regarded by it as treasonable, this form of parole was probably for its purposes, the most comprehensive. Many of the prisoners accepted some or other of the terms proposed, and were released; others declined to make any concessions whatever—insisting that, as they had been arbitrarily imprisoned, they would not recognize the right, which Mr. LINCOLN claimed, to impose upon them any conditions. It is to those who took and maintained this ground that the ensuing portion of this narrative mainly refers.

One fact, however, concerning the negro servants of the prisoners of war, may be worthy of mention. There were with the officers, who were taken at Fort Hatteras, three negroes, two of whom were slaves. At Fort Columbus the Government had offered them their discharge on taking the oath of allegiance, which they had declined. At Fort Warren the oath was again tendered to them, and again refused. Finally, they were offered their liberty on giving their simple parole not to do anything hostile to the Government. They inquired whether, if they went out on such conditions, they would be furnished with passes to go South. They were told these could not be granted, and they then refused to accept the terms offered them. They were bent on returning to their old homes in North Carolina; and one of them took very high ground in the matter, saying, in reply to an inquiry about his refusal to give his parole, that he "wanted to go out honorable." They subsequently went back to North Carolina with the Fort Hatteras prisoners, when the latter were exchanged.

On the 14th of November a notice was posted in the doorway of our quarters, signed by Mr. SETH C. HAWLEY, apprising us of his intention to visit Fort Warren for the purpose of inquiring what prisoners would take the oath, as a preliminary to the investigation of their several cases. On the following day Mr. HAWLEY appeared, and in pursuance of his purpose, called on the prisoners in their quarters. Almost every one rejected his proposition, many taking occasion to couple with their very unequivocal refusal, expressions of contempt for Mr. HAWLEY and those who sent him.

Several of the Members of the Legislature desiring to put in writing the reasons for their refusal to submit to the conditions which Mr. HAWLEY came to propose, signed and handed to him a paper which Mr. S. T. WALLIS had drawn up as his own answer to the inquiry:

"FORT WARREN, *November* 15*th*, 1861.

"MR. SETH C. HAWLEY,

"SIR:

"A notice signed by you appeared this afternoon, upon the walls of the quarters in which we are confined. We quote it, in full, as follows, viz:

'The undersigned appointed by the Secretary of State, U. S., to examine into the cases of the political prisoners at Fort Warren, desires those prisoners to be prepared, to-morrow, to answer the question whether they would severally be willing to take the oath of allegiance to the Constitution and Government of the United States, if they should be set at liberty. Further inquiry into each case to depend upon the answer. To-morrow there will be an opportunity to answer the question.

(Signed,)   'SETH C. HAWLEY. ·

'FORT WARREN, *November* 14*th*, 1861.'

"We presume we are among those whom you designate as "political prisoners," and supposing that you may call upon us, to-morrow, to answer the inquiry which you have indicated, we desire to furnish our reply in our own language, in order that we may not be misunderstood or misrepresented.

"As we understand your notice, 'further inquiry into each case,' is to depend upon the willingness of the individual to take the oath which you propose; that is to say, that no man's case will be inquired into, unless he first signify his willingness to swear as required. We have now been in confinement for more than two months. We were arrested, without process or form of law, upon the alleged authority of the Secretary of State of the United States, who clearly has no lawful authority, whatever, in the premises. We have been dragged from one fortress of the Government to another, by military force, and have been dealt with in a manner which would have been indecent if we had been convicted felons, instead of free men, accused of no offence against the laws of our country. We have been separated from our homes and families, and exposed to constant suffering and privation, to the injury of health, the prejudice of our interests and good name, and in flagrant violation of every right which we have inherited as American citizens. More than this, as members of the Legislature of Maryland, we have been unlawfully withdrawn from the performance of our official duties, in derogation of the constitutional rights of our State and her people. To tell us, after all this, that our 'case' has not even been inquired into, thus far, and that it will not even now be made the subject of inquiry, by the Government at whose hands we have suffered so much wrong, unless we will first submit to conditions as unlawful and arbitrary as our arrest and imprisonment, is to offer to each of us an insult, which we should forfeit our self-respect if we did not repel.

"If we are accused of having committed any offence known to the law, we are entitled to be lawfully and publicly charged therewith, and to be tried—not by you, nor by the Secretary of State—but by the constituted tribunals of the District, from which we have been violently and illegally removed. If we have been guilty of no crime against the law, we are entitled to be discharged, without any terms or conditions, and the Secretary of State—if you really represent him —is only visiting us with an additional outrage, by attempting to impose such upon us.

"We are, your obedient servants,

"E. G. Kilbourn,   Wm. G. Harrison,
S. Teackle Wallis,   Henry M. Warfield,
T. Parkin Scott,   J. Hanson Thomas."

The reasons which influenced the parties to the foregoing document were the same that operated upon all those who declined to make any compromise with the Administration. We still felt, in addition to our own sense of personal wrong, that the cause of constitutional liberty in our State was at stake, and that, as far as our efforts would avail, we were bound to defend it. A refusal to acquiesce in the proceedings by which the Government had outraged the people of Maryland, was the only mode of resisting arbitrary power that was left to us, and we had no hesitation in adhering to our course. But while we, in Fort Warren, were thus endeavoring to discharge what we felt to be our duty in such an exigency, we were hopefully looking to those who were differently situated to support us. Armed resistance on the part of the people of our State would, we well knew, have been utterly vain; but we hoped there would, at least, be a continual and vigorous assertion of their rights from all whose position gave them any influence, or any opportunity of making themselves heard. We thought it possible that when Congress met it might manifest a disposition to compel Mr. LINCOLN to surrender the power he had usurped, and conform thenceforth to the plain dictates of the Constitution and the laws. In this we were disappointed. Some few brave and honest men manfully denounced the course of the Administration, but an overwhelming majority of both Houses, while uttering unmeaning platitudes about our "free Government," our "indestructible constitution," and our "inalienable rights," subserviently supported every despotic and infamous act of Mr. LINCOLN and his advisers. Others held their peace.

About this time, being struck by some paragraphs in a speech delivered, in the Senate, by Mr. TRUMBULL, of Illinois, early in December, 1861, I addressed him the subjoined note :

"FORT WARREN, *December 8th*, 1861.

"HON. LYMAN TRUMBULL, *United States Senate,*

"SIR:

"In the speech delivered by you in the Senate on the 5th inst., I find the following language:' *' The power of Congress to pass a bill of this kind is, to my mind, unquestionable; but I do not place it upon the same ground which has been advanced in some quarters, that in times of war or rebellion, the military is superior to the civil power; or that in such times, what persons may choose to call necessity, is higher than, and above the Constitution. Necessity is the plea of tyrants, and if our Constitution ceases to operate the moment a person charged with its observance thinks there is a necessity to violate it, it is of little value. * * * * * * As unpopular as the avowal may be for the moment among the thoughtless, I here declare that I am for suppressing this monstrous rebellion according to law, and in no other way. * * * * We are fighting to maintain the Constitution, and it especially becomes us, in appealing to the people to come to its rescue, not to violate it ourselves. How are we better than the rebels, if both alike set at nought the Constitution.'* I take leave to recommend these emphatic words to your re-perusal and re-consideration in connection with the following facts. I am a citizen

of the State of Maryland, and, of course of the United States.
On the 12th of September last, I was carried from my house at
midnight, by armed men, who professed to be acting under the orders
of the Secretary of State, but who refused to produce any warrant
whatever in justification of their proceedings. I was carried to Fort
McHenry and have been transferred successively to Fortress Monroe,
Fort La Fayette, and Fort Warren, and am now confined in the
latter. Nearly three months have elapsed since I have been imprisoned, and no charge has been or can be preferred against me, for
I have violated no law, State or Federal. My offence is that I have
denied the justice and policy of the present war, and that I have
insisted on the right of Maryland to ally herself with either section in
the event of the dissolution of the Union—the final destruction of the
political system which she aided to establish. I have expressed
political opinions in opposition to those entertained at Washington,
and for this I am now in prison. Now I presume that you have some
regard for the rights of each and every one of your fellow citizens,
and for your own reputation likewise, and that after the language I
have quoted, and the facts I have referred to, you cannot refuse to
call public attention to my case, and to denounce, from your place in
the Senate, the wrongs that have been done me and scores of my
fellow prisoners. If you expect a future generation to vindicate your
reputation for integrity, it is absolutely necessary that you should
intervene publicly in behalf of men who have been made the victims
of just such arbitrary and unconstitutional measures as you have pro-
tested against. I trust it is not too much for me to anticipate that
your action in this matter will be such as your avowed opinions have
led me to look for.

" I am, very respectfully,

"F. K. HOWARD."

Mr. TRUMBULL did not "call public attention to my case;"
but a few days afterwards he did introduce in the Senate
a resolution calling on the Secretary of State for information as to whether he had caused the arrest of any individuals in the various States, and if so, for what cause.
This resolution was advocated, by Mr. TRUMBULL and one
or two others, with vigor and ability, but was referred to
one of the Standing Committees, and never heard of more.
Mr. TRUMBULL, apparently, soon ceased to trouble himself
about the matter.

To the course of our own Representatives in Congress
we looked with great anxiety. I must frankly say, that
we did expect them to take ground publicly against the
usurpations of the President. We cared less, far less,
about any private effort on their part to extricate us from
the situation in which we were placed, than we did for
some outspoken vindication of the rights of the State of
Maryland—some open denunciation of the wrongs which
had been done her people. Under the influence of these
feelings, I wrote to two of the Representatives of our State,
Mr. MAY, of the House, and Mr. PEARCE, of the Senate.
I had heard that Mr. MAY desired to comment, in his place,
upon the course of the Government, but was restrained by
the conviction that our chances of release would be thereby
damaged. I accordingly wrote to him :

"FORT WARREN, *January 11th*, 1862.

"DEAR SIR:—

"It has been reported here that you have hitherto refrained
from expressing, in Congress, your views upon the situation of Maryland, lest any public effort to aid or vindicate us should result to our
disadvantage. As I am one of the parties interested, permit me to
assure you that I desire no such consideration for me to influence any
man's course. On the contrary, I conceive it to be the duty of each
and every citizen of Maryland, at all times and in all places, to lift
up his voice against the arbitrary proceedings of the Administration,
and to denounce the wrongs done us, be the consequences what they
may. At all events, allow me to say, that I shall never be the one
to complain of such a course on your part, however severely it may
be visited on me by those in power. I write this because, having
heard the rumor in question, I desire to make my own position perfectly clear.   Respectfully, yours,

"F. K. HOWARD.

"HON. HENRY MAY, *Washington, D. C.*"

To this letter I received no reply, but Mr. MAY referred
to it in a letter to Colonel KANE, which he requested him
to inform me of, and said :

"I am solely governed by public considerations, as I ought to be, and of such a nature that, being founded on my own sense of duty, Howard can neither release me from them, nor can ———— wish me to yield them up for any consideration personal to him or myself."

I immediately wrote again to Mr. MAY:

"FORT WARREN, *February 9th*, 1862.

"MY DEAR SIR :—

"Colonel KANE has just shown me a letter, in which, referring to the note I addressed you some time since, you say that you are actuated by 'public considerations,' founded on your own sense of duty, from which I cannot release you. I am somewhat surprised that you should have so far misapprehended the tenor of my note. You will recollect that I simply expressed the wish that, in discharging what I conceived to be your duty, you should not be influenced by the fear that the consequences of your action might be visited on us. So far from assuming to release you from any obligations your sense of duty imposed on you, I merely desired to free you from those personal considerations which I heard had, up to that time, prevented you from discharging a public duty most thoroughly. We did differ perhaps about the nature of the public duty which, in this crisis, has devolved upon you, and the manner in which it should be met. If I had thought we could have so differed, I would probably have refrained from referring to the subject. But I did suppose, considering your own late experiences and our position, and the relations existing between you and us, that but one path was open to you. I did imagine that we would agree upon the proposition that it became Marylanders to resist and denounce the despotism established among us, rather than wait until the evil might correct itself, or be overthrown by others. I am, therefore, for the first time, apprised of my error and thus hasten to explain it. Permit me also to say that as I did not expect any immediate personal advantage to accrue to me from the course I hoped our representatives would pursue in Congress, I was animated by no such considerations when I wrote to you. On the contrary, I thought it possible that such efforts to vindicate our rights might redound to our disadvantage, but I preferred to see the liberties and honor of my State boldly vindicated, even if I paid the penalty. These are still my views, and time will, I am confident, confirm their propriety and justice.

"I remain, very respectfully yours,

"F. K. HOWARD.

"HON. HENRY MAY, *Washington, D. C.*"

Between the dates of the foregoing letters, I wrote also to Senator PEARCE, of Maryland.

"FORT WARREN, *January* 24, 1862.

"DEAR SIR:—

"As one of the Representatives of Maryland in the United States Senate, I take the liberty of calling your attention to the fact that I, with other of my fellow-citizens, am still a prisoner in Fort Warren, Boston Harbor. You are probably familiar, as is the whole civilized world, with the circumstances under which so many gentlemen of our State have been dragged from their homes and imprisoned by order of the general Government. It may not be amiss, however, to refer to the manner and causes of my arrest and detention. A little after midnight on the 12th of September last, I was seized in my own house by a band of armed men, who professed to be acting under the orders of Mr. WM. H. SEWARD, but who showed no warrant whatever for their proceedings. The indignities to which I was subjected, and the painful scenes consequent upon that outrage, I need not detail to you. Suffice it to say, that my house was searched from garret to cellar, my private papers were examined and carried off, and I was sent to Fort McHenry. From that place I was transferred successively to Fortress Monroe, Fort Lafayette, and Fort Warren, and at each of these Posts I have been kept a close prisoner, and have received the treatment of a common prisoner of war. It is proper that I should say to you that I have not in any way whatever, violated any law, State or Federal. I was one of the editors of the *Daily Exchange*, and expressed through the columns of that journal, opinions at variance with those entertained by the Administration. I opposed the war upon the South, and this I had an indisputable right to do. I argued that it would only render the separation of the two sections more certain, that it would leave us burthened with a fearful debt, and that it would demoralize both Government and people, and lead us insensibly towards a despotism or anarchy. These views also I had the right to entertain and utter. Such is the sum total of my offences ; and for such cause have I been held a close prisoner for more than four months under an arbitrary order of a member of the Cabinet. My business is in all probability ruined, and I leave you to conjecture what distress my family has suffered. In this matter my rights and the liberties of my native State have been alike contemptuously violated. Now, it seems to me, sir, that a Representative of Maryland has but one clear line of duty to pursue, and that is, to denounce persistently and boldly the usurpations of the Executive. I am aware of the fact that you have more than once expressed your views upon this subject, on the floor of the Senate, but it has been when the topic was started by other Senators. Our Representatives have only played subordinate parts, in debates which others initiated and chiefly sustained. I am not aware that you or your colleagues have challenged the attention of the country to the wrongs done us, or have made any public or detailed statement in regard to individual cases here, of which there are many well calculated to arrest the attention and awaken the indignation of the people. Such a course might not, it is true, be productive of practical results to us, but it is, if you will permit me to say so, the path which I think it becomes those public men to follow who have been educated as, and are worthy of the name of American freemen.

Whatever might happen to individuals, the principles which underlie our Government, would thus be vindicated, and they can be manfully vindicated, at present, in no other way.

"I have written to you more plainly than you may perhaps think warrantable. But I feel that I need offer no apology for so doing — I have been subjected to personal outrage and political degradation. You are a representative of Maryland and have a high, and it may be a dangerous duty to discharge; for as a citizen of that State, I have a right to ask that you should even jeopard your liberty in defence of mine, and that you should uphold, even though it be in an unavailing struggle, the honor of our State. This I do, and I trust that in dealing thus frankly with this question, I have not uttered anything that is otherwise than personally respectful to you. If so, I have done violence to my own feelings and intentions, but I have too much at stake to hesitate to speak with perfect candor.

"I remain, very respectfully,

"Your obedient servant,

"F. K. HOWARD.

"Hon. James A. Pearce, U. S. Senate, *Washington, D. C.*"

Receiving no answer, I again wrote to Mr. Pearce:

"Fort Warren, *February* 27*th*, 1862.

"Dear Sir :—

"On the 24th ult. I addressed you a letter from this place, but, as the regulations of the post-office are somewhat stringent in

10

these days, I am in doubt as to whether my letter ever reached you.
Will you be good enough to let me know whether you received it?
I do not write to solicit a reply to its contents, but only to get the
information I have herein requested.

" Respectfully, yours,

"F. K. HOWARD.

" HON. JAMES A. PEARCE, *Washington, D. C.*"

About a week afterwards I received this answer from Mr.
PEARCE:

"SENATE, 5*th March*, 1862.

" DEAR SIR:—

" I acknowledge the receipt of your letter of the 27th February, and of the former one to which you allude. That letter I did not
answer for more reasons than one. An indisposition from which I
have long suffered, makes writing difficult and painful to me, and, as
I was engaged in earnest efforts to procure the release of yourself and
other gentlemen illegally and unjustly detained, as I think, I thought
it best not to write till I could communicate fully. There was
another reason. You seemed to think that, though I had on several
occasions expressed my opinions freely as to these arrests, and had
strongly condemned them, there was something else that I ought to
have done, but had omitted to do. What this was you did not say,
but you intimated that it was a high and might be a dangerous duty.
What that duty was I could only infer from your remark, that what I
had said in this Senate was but incidental only. Any direct proposition submitted by me would not, I think, be dangerous to me. And
were it so, I trust I should not be deterred from the discharge of a
duty by fear of consequences to myself.

" But I am satisfied that no benefit to you, and to gentlemen alike
unjustly confined, as I think, can be secured by any movement made
by me in the Senate.

" There is a disposition on the part of the Administration to relax
these rigors towards all so situated.

" But, at this time, I feel that I can neither benefit those I wish to
serve, or promote sound doctrine on this subject, by any proceedings
of mine. Mr. TRUMBULL's resolution was sent to the committee on
the judiciary to be there entombed, and I doubt whether any resolution by me would be allowed to be discussed. But I shall watch for

any opportunity of changed feelings or altered circumstances, which will afford the least promise of doing anything useful in this respect. Mr. Brown has been kept in confinement, I am sure, for fear that his release would complicate the police question in Baltimore. Most of the gentlemen with you, I know and esteem highly. They have my warmest sympathies, nor would I hesitate to pursue any practicable plan which promised to secure their release.

"Very respectfully and truly yours,

"J. A. PEARCE.

"F. K. HOWARD, Esq."

I have reproduced these letters simply to illustrate fully our views. They will show how anxious we were that the great principles which we were endeavoring to uphold, at such a cost to us, should be vindicated by those whose position enabled them to command, at least for a moment, the attention of the country. The gentlemen whom I had thus addressed thought a different course best and wisest; but, however that may be, their decision was certainly deeply regretted by all the "political prisoners" from Maryland in Fort Warren.

In the early part of February we learned through the newspapers that we had been transferred from the custody of the State Department to that of the War Department. Very soon afterwards a lengthy Proclamation signed by Mr. STANTON appeared in the newspapers. It was dated February 14th, 1862, and was entitled "Executive Order in Relation to State Prisoners, No. 1." This Order contained a summary of Mr. STANTON's views and opinions upon the revolution in the Southern States, its course and probable results, and upon the action of the Federal Government, and concluded thus:

"The insurrection is believed to have culminated and to be declining. The President in view of these facts, and anxious to favor a return to the normal course of the administration, as far as a regard for the public welfare will allow, directs that all political prisoners or State prisoners now held in military custody be released on their subscribing a parole engaging them to render no aid or comfort to enemies in hostility to the United States. The Secretary of War will, however, in his discretion, except from the effects of this order, any persons detained as spies in the service of the insurgents, or others whose release at the present moment may be deemed incompatible with the public safety.

To all persons who shall be so released, and shall keep their parole, the President grants an amnesty for any past offences of treason or disloyalty which they may have committed. Extraordinary arrests will hereafter be made under the direction of the military authorities alone.

"By order of the President.

"EDWIN M. STANTON,

"*Secretary of War.*"

Shortly afterwards the following Order was also promulgated by the Secretary of War:

"OFFICIAL.

"*Executive Order, No. 2, in Relation to the State Prisoners.*

"WAR DEPARTMENT, Washington City, *Feb.* 27*th*, 1862.

"It is ordered:—

"*First*—That a special commission of two persons,—one of military rank and the other in civil life,—be appointed to examine the cases of the State prisoners remaining in the military custody of the United States, and to determine whether, in view of the public safety and the existing rebellion, they should be discharged, or remain in military custody, or be remitted to the civil tribunals for trial.

"*Second*—That Major General JOHN A. DIX, commanding in Baltimore, and the Hon. EDWARDS PIERRPONT, of New York, be and they are hereby appointed commissioners for the purposes above mentioned, and they are authorized to examine, hear and determine the cases aforesaid, *ex parte*, and in a summary manner, at such times and places as in their discretion they may appoint, and make full report to the War Department.

"By order of the President.

"EDWIN M. STANTON,

"*Secretary of War.*

After the Proclamation of February 14th, was issued, Colonel DIMICK was authorized to release a number of persons upon their signing a parole not to give " aid or comfort to the enemies in hostility to the United States ;" and some weeks after the appointment of Mr. STANTON's commission, orders were received for the release of other parties upon the same conditions. A number still refused to accept the proffered terms. Two of them, Messrs. WM. H. GATCHELL and WM. G. HARRISON, gave their reasons for so refusing, in the following letters to Mr. STANTON :

"FORT WARREN, *February 22d,* 1862.

"HON. E. M. STANTON, *Secretary of War,*

"SIR :

" I have been arrested and imprisoned for nearly eight months, in violation of the Constitution and Laws of the United States, having *never* committed any offence against either.

"I am not, in any legitimate sense, the subject of an amnesty. That, as I have always understood, is an offer of pardon *by the offended to the offending party.* The proclamation and the parole are to be taken together, and they reverse the order of things.

"I cannot consent to any terms, which even seem to justify the action of the Government towards me, or will place me in any different condition from all other free citizens.

" Your obedient servant,

"WM. H. GATCHELL."

___

"FORT WARREN, *February* 22, 1862.

"HON. EDWIN M. STANTON, *Secretary of War.*

"SIR :—

" As a member of the Legislature of Maryland, I was taken from my dwelling house, at midnight of the 12th of September last, by the military police of the city of Baltimore, and have since been incarcerated in several prisons, and now nearly four months in this one, Fort Warren. I was told my arrest was by orders from Washington. I refuse any release, except an unconditional one, because I

will not seem even to acquiesce in an act, which has violated one of
the most sacred bonds of our Government, (vide Article 4th, Amend-
ments to the Constitution.) I have been arrested in defiance of law,
punished without charge of crime, or trial, and judgment of my
peers, and I will not sanction the insinuation which a parole affords,
that any charge has been made or proved, warranting what has been
done.

" Respectfully,   •

" W. G. HARRISON."

As I saw, from the Proclamation and Order of the new
Secretary of War, that he intended to deal with us arbitrarily, instead of justly, I did not think it necessary to
await propositions which I could not accept, and which
might not even be offered to me. I had never made any
statement of my wrongs, nor had I individually forwarded
any remonstrance against my arrest to the Government, and
I therefore took that occasion to put my case upon the records
of the Department, and sent this letter to Mr. STANTON :

" FORT WARREN, MASS., March 3d, 1862.

" HON. EDWIN M. STANTON, <i>Sec'y of War,</i>

   " SIR :

    " For six months past I have been detained in close custody in
one or other of the Forts of the United States. I am, I believe,
termed, in the novel language of the day, a " political prisoner," or
" prisoner of State." Until recently I have been held subject to the
order of the Secretary of State, but I now understand that I am specially in charge of the War Department. You, therefore, are responsible for my further detention. Under these circumstances it is
proper that I should place upon record, in your office, a statement of
the wrongs done me, and a demand for an instant and unconditional
release.

    " On the night of the 12th of September, 1861, between 12 and 1
o'clock, I was made prisoner in my own house, in Baltimore, by a band
of armed men, who, although they showed no warrant or authority for
their proceedings, professed, and I have no doubt truly, to be acting
under the orders of Mr. SEWARD, the Secretary of State. My house
was searched from garret to cellar—my private papers ransacked, and

most of them, as far as I can learn, were carried off. I was kept for
an hour or more a prisoner in my own parlor—armed men being stationed throughout my house, and even at the door of my children's
chamber while this search was proceeding. I will not comment further upon the indignities then put upon me. I was finally carried off
to Fort McHenry, leaving my house in possession of the myrmidons
who had invaded it, and who refused to allow me to send for my wife's
father or brother, who were in the immediate neighborhood, and to
whom alone my family, at such a moment, could look for protection.
I was detained at Fort McHenry during the following day, and then
transferred to Fortress Monroe. At this latter post I was confined a
close prisoner, with fourteen other gentlemen, for ten days, none of us
having been suffered to leave for an instant the two casemates which
were there assigned to us. So rigid was our imprisonment, that the
very windows and doors, through which we could look out on the parade ground, were closed and padlocked. I was then carried, with my
companions, to Fort La Fayette. At this latter Post no provision whatever had been made for our reception, and no decent accommodations
were at any time provided. I slept in the dark, cold gun-battery, in
which I was quartered, upon a bag of straw until I procured bedding
from New York; and during my whole stay I was compelled to pay
for my meals, as I could not have eaten the wretched rations offered
me by the commanding officer. On the 1st of November last I was
brought to this place on an over-crowded and filthy steamer, which
was insufficiently supplied even with the miserable pork and bread provided for our subsistence. But for the fact that I had brought my bedding with me, I should have been forced, like many of my companions,
to sleep for two weeks after my arrival here upon the bare floor, and
without a single blanket to cover me. Such is a brief statement of
the treatment to which I have been subjected.

"From the moment of my arrest down to this hour no charge of
any sort has been preferred against me, and none can be alleged or
established, for I have not violated any law whatever, State or Federal.
I was, as you may perhaps be aware, one of the Editors of the Daily
Exchange, a morning journal published in Baltimore. In that paper
I had expressed my political opinions without reserve. I had, a year
ago, advocated the adoption of some compromise by Congress which
should stay the then threatened rupture between the North and South.
I had subsequently deprecated any attempt to coerce the South, on the
ground that it would only render the separation of the two sections inevitable and final. I asserted that war would leave the country in a worse
condition than it found it; and, as it would entail upon us an enor-

mous debt, I felt it to be my duty to resist, and I did resist its initiation. I was unable to see how the Union could be preserved if a large majority of the Southern people were bent upon a separation, and I said so. I was unable to comprehend how the President could, from the injunction which commanded him to see that the laws were faithfully executed, derive authority to supersede and violate the fundamental laws of the land, and I said so. I was equally unable to see how, upon the theory of upholding the Constitution, I was under an obligation to support those who were daily manifesting their contempt for all its provisions—nor could I conceive how this Government had any existence whatever outside of the charter which established it. All these political opinions I had the absolute right to entertain and promulgate. I choose to refer to them here, because they constitute the offences for which I am undergoing punishment. Notwithstanding the fact that many thousands of persons in the Northern States had entertained and expressed these views within a twelve-month, the Administration determined that it was criminal in me to continue to hold and utter them, and has, therefore, arbitrarily inflicted upon me the indignities and wrongs which I have mentioned.

"Although no direct offer has been made to me to release me upon any terms whatsoever, I, nevertheless, presume that mine was one of the cases which, either your Proclamation of February 14th, or your Order of February 27th, was intended to cover. Now, as I cannot accept a conditional discharge, coupled with a gracious amnesty for offences which it is assumed I have committed, and as I must equally refuse to appear at the bar of an irresponsible tribunal to justify my right to the ordinary privileges of a citizen of Maryland, it is due to myself, at least, that I should state the reasons which impel me to the course I shall pursue. To the principles which govern my action now I shall appeal, when in the future I seek redress and enter upon my own vindication. It must be obvious to you, Sir, that I cannot, consistently with my own self-respect, accept any such conditional release as is referred to in your Proclamation, or avail myself of such amnesty. As I was despotically deprived of my freedom, I can make no compromise to regain it. As I am punished merely for venturing to dissent from the theories and policy of the Administration, I need and will ask no pardon. Nor, even if I should accept the terms mentioned, would I have any security that I would not, immediately after my release, be again subjected to precisely similar outrages to those which have already been inflicted upon me. As the Administration has once determined that I, by expressing my political sentiments, was giving 'aid and comfort to the enemies in hostility to the United States,' I could only escape a re-arrest by consenting to forego or conceal my opinions. This I will never, for one instant, do. I deem it to be my bounden duty to defend, to the last, every privilege and right to which, as an American citizen, I was born; and I shall do so until I am deprived of these by some known and fair process of law.

"Nor can you fail readily to comprehend why I decline to submit myself to the jurisdiction of the strange tribunal which is organized under your order of February 27th. I recognize no such judges of my guilt or innocence, of my loyalty or disloyalty, under the Constitution or laws of this land. The courts, both State and Federal, are in the unobstructed exercise of their several functions in Maryland; and they could long since have examined and disposed of any charge which might have been preferred against me. In them, and in them only, will I meet any accusation; and, while they are closed to my demand for justice, I shall decline to defend myself before any Star-Chamber commissioners whomsoever.

"Such, Sir, are the motives of my present action; and as the rights which I seek to uphold are not dependent upon the alleged necessities of the Administration, or upon the fate of battles, my convictions can not be affected by the supposed exigencies of the one, or the results of the other. I shall continue, then, to vindicate them, as I best may, with the consciousness that, after the delusions, the falsehoods, and the passions of the hour shall have passed away, my course will be approved by every honest man who has been educated in the knowledge of the privileges and duties of an American freeman. I have only now to demand, at your hands, a prompt release from the imprisonment to which I am so unjustly and arbitrarily subjected.

"I remain

"Your obedient servant,

"F. K. HOWARD."

The only notice taken of this communication was the following note from the Adjutant-General:

"WAR DEPARTMENT,

"WASHINGTON CITY, D. C., *March* 10*th*, 1862.

" To COLONEL JUSTIN DIMICK, *Fort Warren*,

"BOSTON, MASSACHUSETTS.

"COLONEL:

" I will thank you to inform Mr. FRANK KEY HOWARD, that his letter of the 3d instant has been duly received, and that his case has been referred to the Commissioners named in the within order.

" By order of the Secretary of War.

"L. THOMAS,

"*Adjutant General.*"

With this letter was forwarded a printed copy of Mr. STANTON's order of February 27th. The views of all those who had refused to accept any conditional discharge were, in the main, those set forth in the above letter to Mr. STANTON.

Our time at Fort Warren, as at our previous places of imprisonment, passed as may be supposed, monotonously enough. Living as we did in overcrowded apartments, it was impossible to read or write with any satisfaction. Restricted as we were for many months to our quarters or to a narrow strip of ground in front of them, we could derive little pleasure from exercising in the open air. To pace up and down within these contracted limits, where nothing was to be seen but the dull, gray walls of our prison was not a cheerful or invigorating mode of exercise. As month after month dragged wearily on, our hopes of release grew fainter and fainter, and though we seldom permitted ourselves to talk despondingly to each other, we did not think the less bitterly about the homes we had left and the indignities we had endured.

At Fort Warren the soldiers of the garrison differed, we were glad to find, from their comrades at Fort La Fayette. While the latter were incapable of delivering a message or of giving the simplest order, save in a manner at once insolent and brutal, the former were uniformly good-natured and civil. COL. DIMICK, the Commandant of the Post discharged his disagreeable office in a way to which we could take no exception, and none of us in any interview with him ever found him otherwise than courteous and kind. As far as lay in his power he left nothing undone to promote our comfort.

On the 19th of April an order was issued giving us permission to walk, between 1 o'clock, P. M., and sunset, upon that portion of the ramparts immediately over our quarters. The space thus assigned us was just the length of that to which we had been limited upon the parade ground, that is, about three hundred feet. This extension of our bounds was an infinite relief to us, as from the ramparts we had a view of the bay and the surrounding shores.

The unwillingness of the War and State Departments to grant passes to persons desirous of visiting any prisoner, may be judged from the following note from Mr. SEWARD to REV. MR. HITSELBERGER, a Catholic priest residing in Boston. He had applied, at the request of Mr. T. PARKIN SCOTT, for a permit to enable him, as a priest, to visit the latter, and received this reply:

"DEPARTMENT OF STATE,
"WASHINGTON, *Nov. 20th,* 1861.
"To the REV. A. L. HITSELBERGER,
"BOSTON COLLEGE, Harrison Avenue, Boston.
"SIR:

"I have to acknowledge the receipt of your note of the 15th instant, with a copy of that which you addressed to COL. DIMICK, on the 15th of November. This Department having adopted a rule which precludes all visits to political prisoners, even from Ministers of the Gospel—of any denomination—has hitherto strictly observed it.

If, however, the persons themselves shall in the event of sickness, or any other reasonable cause, require the services of their spiritual advisers, the rule would be relaxed in favor of any one of undoubted loyalty. "I am Sir,
"Your obedient servant,
"WILLIAM H. SEWARD."

It was not until April that MR. HITSELBERGER succeeded in obtaining a pass to visit Fort Warren.

Genl. DIX and Judge PIERREPONT, who had been appointed Commissioners to examine the cases of "State Prisoners" by Mr. STANTON's order of February 27th, arrived at Fort Warren, May 7th, 1862. They were engaged about five hours in disposing of these "cases." Their "examination" consisted in asking one or two simple questions no way touching any crime or offence known to the laws, and in offering to release, on parole, most of the parties called before them. Several persons were released on some special grounds which distinguished their "cases" from those of the strictly "political prisoners," who unanimously rejected the proposals of the Commissioners. The latter did not attempt to say that the Government had any specific charges to prefer against those on whom it wished to impose conditions. That these prisoners had been confined simply because their opinions were in opposition to those of the members and partisans of the Administration, was tacitly conceded by the Commissioners in their so-called examination.

The following is a memorandum of the interview between Mr. WM. H. GATCHELL and Mr. STANTON'S Commissioners. It was drawn up by Mr. GATCHELL a few hours after his "examination."

"As I entered the room in which the Commissioners held their meeting, Genl. DIX advanced with his hand extended, saying, 'good morning, Mr. GATCHELL.' I declined the proffered hand, remarking, 'excuse me, Sir, if you please.' In a very short time, Judge PIERREPONT observed, 'I really forget, Mr. GATCHELL, whether you have been offered the parole or not, heretofore.' I replied, that 'I had been and that I had declined it, for the reasons stated in my answer to the Secretary of War, which I supposed he had seen.' He said he 'had not seen that answer.' I told him that 'I would furnish the Commissioners with a copy, that they might understand the grounds on which I placed my refusal to accept it.' I was then asked, 'whether I continued of the same mind?' I answered, 'certainly.' Then, said he, 'for the present, we have nothing more to do with your case.'

"I then turned to General DIX and said: 'At the time we left Fort McHenry for Fort La Fayette, you, Sir, assured our families and ourselves that our treatment there should be as comfortable, if not more so, than at Fort McHenry; instead of which, for the first thirty days we were there, we were treated like brutes—that, but for the fact of our having taken our bedding with us, we should have been obliged to sleep upon the bare floor, and for fifteen days we had not a chair to sit upon.' He said, 'I could not know what the condition of things was at La Fayette.' I replied, 'You ought to have known before you made the promise, particularly as we were sent there by your orders.' He then said, 'Mr. GATCHELL, nobody knows better than you that what I did was by orders from my Government. 'Yes,' I replied, 'but, as Commander of a Military Department, those orders must have been suggested by you, or adopted with your advice and consent.'"

The reasons why the gentlemen then in Fort Warren refused to give the required parole, have already been adverted to. Four of us: Messrs. SCOTT, WALLIS, my father and myself, whom the Government had not, openly—or secretly, so far as we knew—charged with any illegal act, were not summoned before the Commissioners. Our "cases" were therefore not "examined," nor were we offered our liberty on any terms. Col. KANE, against whom the Government had managed to procure an indictment for treason, and who had been carried out of the State immediately afterwards, remained unnoticed, also. He had been removed hundreds of miles away from the place where it was alleged he had committed a crime, and though for nine months the Government had failed to bring him to trial, the Commissioners suffered his case, also, to pass unexamined. To Mr. BROWN, the Mayor of Baltimore, Gen. Dix said that all parties in Baltimore bore testimony to his personal integrity and that the Government recognized his fidelity in his intercourse with it, and he then offered to release him, provided he would resign his office. Mr. BROWN replied that he was in the power of the Government and submitted only because he could not help himself, but he peremptorily refused Gen. DIX's proposition to resign his office, remarking that to do so would be to forfeit his own self-respect. Comment on this infamous and insolent proposal is needless.

An article which appeared in the Baltimore *American* on the 15th of May, furnished conclusive evidence of the spirit in which the Commissioners had acted. The principal editor and proprietor of that journal was Mr. CHARLES C. FULTON, a man who had been for years the apologist of every species of fraud and violence which had been perpetrated to advance the ends and interests of his party or himself, and who was at that time the subservient dependant of Gen. DIX and Gen. DIX's master. As his account of the visit of the former to Fort Warren was mainly correct, so far as the facts therein stated were concerned, it may be fairly presumed that he received it from one of the Commissioners or their clerk. In that article it was said :

"We understand that the prisoners not examined were Messrs. S. TEACKLE WALLIS, T. PARKIN SCOTT, CHARLES HOWARD, F. KEY HOWARD, and GEORGE P. KANE, all of this city. The reason why no examination was made in these cases is understood to have been the conviction, on the part of the Commissioners, that they ought not to be permitted to return to Baltimore, on any condition, while the class of citizens here of which they are a type keep up an unrelenting hostility to the Government—provoking, most justly, a hostile feeling towards them on the part of the Union men of this city. * * * That the feeling of hostility to which we have alluded has been fostered and embittered by the vindictiveness of the Secession women of Baltimore there can be no doubt; and to them is due—in a great degree, at least—as prime movers of disloyalty, the continued imprisonment of their friends.

It is manifest, from these extracts, that the "hostile feeling" of Mr. LINCOLN's partisans towards us was one of the reasons why the outrage done us remained unredressed; and a disposition to inflict vicarious punishment on the women of Baltimore was another of the manly and just motives operating upon General DIX. On May the 9th, Colonel DIMICK enlarged our bounds. We had permission from that time to walk where we pleased, both inside and outside of the fortress, on giving our parole not to attempt to pass beyond the line of sentinels who were stationed along the shore. Our parole also required us not to communicate with the shore, or with any one who might land on the island, and not to talk to the soldiers of the garrison, or to discuss political matters in their hearing.

On Saturday, May 24th, Colonel DIMICK notified us that the "political prisoners" were to be sent back to Fort La Fayette. We regarded this as indicating a determination on the part of the Government to subject us to all such indignities or punishment as it was in its power to inflict. That the Government itself considered Fort La Fayette as peculiarly a place of punishment, was made evident by an order which was received at the same time for the transfer of certain other persons to the same Fortress. A number of prisoners of war, who had been taken in the battle below New Orleans, had reached Fort Warren but two days before. Among them were six officers of the steam-battery Louisiana, which they had blown up rather than suffer it to fall into the hands of the Federal forces. For this reason the Government chose to regard them as meriting severe treatment. On their arrival, they, like all other Confederate officers, were allowed the liberty of the Island upon their parole. With the order for our transfer to Fort La Fayette came another directing that these officers should not be regarded as, nor receive the ordinary treatment of prisoners of war, and that they should be sent to Fort La Fayette with us. Their parole was instantly revoked and they were placed under all the restrictions to which we had so long been subjected. It was thus made manifest that the Government was fully aware of the specially painful character of the imprisonment which the unhappy captives in Fort La Fayette were compelled to endure.

On Monday, the 26th, Colonel DIMICK received a dispatch informing him that Fort La Fayette was already full to repletion, and ordering him to retain us for the time at Fort Warren. That morning the public had been made aware of the fact that General BANKS had been driven by General JACKSON across the Potomac in great confusion. A special dispatch had been received at Fort Warren to the same effect, during the previous night, and the garrison left that day in great haste for Washington. Probably the Government had, for some time, more important matters to think about than the punishment of "political prisoners," for we heard no more of any orders for our removal. On Thursday, July 31st, the prisoners of war then in Fort Warren, some two hundred in number, left on a steamer for James River, where they were to be exchanged. After their departure there were but fourteen "political prisoners" left in Fort Warren.

On the 25th of October, a petition for a writ of Habeas Corpus in behalf of Mr. WM. H. WINDER was filed in the United States Circuit Court in Boston. Judge CLIFFORD, one of the Judges of the United States Supreme Court, ordered the writ to be issued. The Marshal declined to serve it. It was then placed in the hands of one of the Sheriff's officers. The officer endeavored to reach the fort on the boat which was in the service of the Government, but was refused a passage, unless he could get an order from Colonel DIMICK, or the War Department. He then hired a sail-boat and attempted to communicate with the fort; but a vigilant lookout was kept, and he was warned off by the sentinels. He was utterly unable to serve it; and thus ended this attempt to release a "political prisoner" from Fort Warren through process of law.

On the afternoon of the 12th of November, my father received a telegraphic despatch, informing him of the "extreme illness" of my sister. At the same time, Colonel DIMICK notified him that he was authorized to release him upon his parole to return to Fort Warren at the expiration of a limited period, and to commit no act of hostility in the meantime against the Government. This was one of those few cases in which we had all agreed that it would be our duty to accept a temporary release. Colonel DIMICK desired to extend this parole to thirty days; but my father stated his unwillingness to remain in Baltimore, under any conditions whatsoever, any longer than might be absolutely necessary, and gave a parole, therefore, to return to Fort Warren in twenty days. The friends who had procured for him this temporary release had applied for one for me also, but of this application no notice was taken. Had I been then permitted, I should have thought it proper for me to go home. On the evening of the 14th I received a message from my father, dated in the morning, informing me that my sister's end was rapidly approaching. At the same time COL. DIMICK told me he was authorized to release me on parole. I subsequently learned that this order to him was the result of a renewed application on my behalf. But it came too late, and there were no longer any reasons moving me to take advantage of it, save such as were purely personal to myself. A few moments reflection satisfied me that, under such circumstances, I ought not to deviate from my course. I therefore declined to accept the temporary and conditional release which Mr. STANTON had so tardily offered me. While my father was at home COL. DIMICK proposed to extend the time of his stay indefinitely, and to receive his simple pledge to return to Fort Warren when so ordered, without exacting from him any other conditions whatsoever, thus leaving him, in all other respects, perfect freedom of action. My father declined, however, to take into consideration any further proposition looking to his discharge, temporarily or permanently, upon any terms whatsoever, and notified COL. DIMICK that he would be at Fort Warren on the 3d of December, the day when his parole would expire.

On the 24th of November an order of the War Department, dated Nov. 22d., relating to the discharge of prisoners who had been arrested for interfering with the draft, &c., appeared in the Boston papers. Though the order did not refer directly to persons in our situation, still there was so much ambiguity in its language that it was not clear whether it might not be intended to include us. On the same afternoon, Col. DIMICK received this dispatch :

" WASHINGTON, *Nov.* 24*th*, 11.50 A. M.

" COMMANDING OFFICER, Fort Warren, Boston.

" None of the prisoners confined at your Post will be released under order of the War Department of the 22d instant, without

12

special instructions from the Department. By order of the Secretary of War.

"E. D. TOWNSEND.

"*A. A. G.*"

I had not myself thought that the order of November 22d would affect us, though some of my companions were of a different opinion.   The above dispatch to Colonel Dimick effectually banished from the minds of most of them any doubts upon the point.

Late in the afternoon of the 26th of November, 1862, Colonel Dimick entered our quarters and, with a manifestation of much pleasure and good feeling, announced to us that our captivity was ended.   He had just received a telegram from Washington ordering our release and containing no suggestion about terms or conditions.   He furnished us the next morning, at our request, with the following certificate :

"Fort Warren, Boston Harbor,
"November 27th, 1862.

"George P. Kane,
"George Wm. Brown,
"Charles Howard,
"Frank K. Howard,
"Henry M. Warfield,
"William G. Harrison,
"Robert Hull,
"S. Teackle Wallis,
"Charles Macgill,
"William Gatchell,
"Thomas W. Hall,
"T. Parkin Scott,
"William H. Winder.

"The above named prisoners are released agreeably to the following telegram.

"J. Dimick, *Col. 1st Art'y Com. Post.*

'WASHINGTON, *Nov.* 26*th*, 1862.

' COL. J. DIMICK, U. S. Army, Fort Warren, Boston:

'The Secretary of War directs that you release all the Maryland State prisoners, also any other prisoners that may be in your custody and report names to this office.

'Signed,   'E. D. TOWNSEND.

A. A. General.

"True copy.

"FORT WARREN, *November* 27*th*, 1862.

"J. DIMICK,

"Col. 1st Art'y, Com'g Post."

———

We left our prison for our homes on the morning of the 27th.

There were, at the time of our release, no other prisoners in Fort Warren than those named, except one, who was a native of Massachusetts, and who had been arrested in that State, a few weeks previously. The gentlemen above named had, with a single exception, been my companions in Fort La Fayette, and of course in Fort Warren. All but one had been imprisoned over a year, and Mr. GATCHELL, Col. KANE and my father for nearly eighteen months. Each of them had determined at the outset to resist, to the uttermost, the dictatorship of ABRAHAM LINCOLN, and having done so, each had the satisfaction of feeling, as he left Fort Warren, that he had faithfully, and not unsuccessfully, discharged a grave public duty. We came out of prison as we had gone in, holding in the same just scorn and detestation the despotism under which the country was prostrate, and with a stronger resolution than ever to oppose it by every means to which, as American freemen, we had the right to resort.

www.ingramcontent.com/pod-product-compliance
Lightning Source LLC
Chambersburg PA
CBHW020258090426
42735CB00009B/1132